Real Food
Treats

Jess Lomas

JESS LOMAS is an author, editor and freelance film reviewer from Melbourne, Australia. Her previous titles include *Diabetes Recipes, Diabetes – Collected Edition, Diabetes – Simple Ideas for Big Change, Low Sugar No Sugar, Low Sugar – Collected Edition, Quit Sugar Quick* and *Sugar Detox*.

Published by:
Wilkinson Publishing Pty Ltd
ACN 006 042 173
Level 4, 2 Collins St Melbourne,
Victoria, Australia 3000
Ph: +61 3 9654 5446
www.wilkinsonpublishing.com.au

International distribution by Pineapple Media Limited
(wwwpineapple-media.com)   ISSN 1838-5389

National Library of Australia Cataloguing-in-Publication entry:

Creator:	Lomas, Jess, author.
Title:	Real food treats / Jess Lomas.
ISBN:	9781925265255 (paperback)
Subjects:	Cooking.
	Cooking (Natural foods)
Dewey Number:	641.563
Layout Design:	Corinda Cook, Tango Media Pty Ltd
Cover Design:	Alicia Freile, Tango Media Pty Ltd

Photos and illustrations by agreement with photo agencies including Getty. Recipe and farmers' market photography by agreement with Jess Lomas.

Contents

Welcome to my Real Food kitchen, thanks for taking the time to visit, I hope you find something in the following pages to inspire you in your own kitchen and life!

Food is central to life, we love to cook it, share it, photograph it and above all eat it. Meals shared around the table with family and friends can be some of the best times we have; recipes passed down through generations always trump new recipes; and perfecting a recipe for the first time is a great feeling.

Today, more than ever, we find ourselves attempting to balance the pleasures of food with our health, as we become increasingly aware of the dangers of excess refined sugar, wheat and highly processed ingredients on our bodies. Rates of disease are reportedly increasing, with type 2 diabetes swiftly becoming a real threat for many families. We battle with weight, energy and immunity, reaching for convenience to fuel our busy lives. Pretty soon many of us are running on empty and asking, what went wrong?

The good and bad news is that while supermarkets are groaning under the weight of packaged goods full of ingredients we can't pronounce, a wide range of healthy alternatives are increasingly becoming available to us. This presents the consumer with the ultimate choice: to follow the leader (Big Food), or take their own path and get back to basics with a Real Food mindset.

As someone who has spent a portion of their life as a picky eater – I still can't stomach bananas – and then as a sugar addict in my late teens and early twenties, my arrival at a Real Food mindset came at a tipping point in my life, when my health could no longer be ignored. I had to do a massive mental overhaul to change how I thought about food, how I felt when I ate food, and how the food I prepared for others might make them feel.

What I discovered by going back to basics was that Real Food tastes good, better than the Big Food alternatives in fact. Real Food lets me get creative and think about nourishing my body in ways that work for me, and not some company's profits. Do I work better in the morning on a bowl of sugary cereal or with a veggie-packed quinoa bowl that gets my daily vegetable count up before I'm even out the door? Do I need to buy a packet of biscuits or cake as a treat when I can whizz up my own concoctions that won't send my blood sugar levels on a rollercoaster ride?

These are questions you may ask yourself, and your answers will be different to mine. You may want to completely overhaul your kitchen and lifestyle, or you may want to take small steps to change some less than desirable aspects of your diet, it's entirely up to you. My hope is that the following recipes give you the much-needed push to get started if you've been debating what to do, or that they add to your growing recipe library if you are already living the Real Food life.

Enjoy!

The Real Food *mindset*

How do you shift from regular eating to Real Food eating?
The process is simpler than you may think,
just ask yourself the below question.

Does the food come more from nature or a factory?

If you're holding a lettuce in one hand and a packet of biscuits in the other, the differences are obvious, as is the better choice. If you're holding a jar of Italian flavoured pasta sauce in one hand and a jar of tomato passata (paste) in the other, it might prove more difficult.

Always go for the product with less ingredients, real food often only has one. Reading the nutritional label on products will help you decide if that jar or packet should go in your trolley or back on the shelves. While checking the sodium and sugar levels can be helpful, I often go straight to the list of ingredients. Here are my three simple rules when considering a product:

1. Avoid products with more than 5 ingredients.

2. Avoid products that list sugar as the first ingredient.

3. Avoid products with ingredients you don't know or can't pronounce.

Taking the step from flavoured pasta sauce to plain tomato paste is good but making your own sauce from fresh tomatoes is great. The next stage of Real Food living, beyond making better choices between packaged foods, is making your own versions of those packaged goods. Once you set your kitchen up with the right tools and ingredients, there's no need to buy sauces, dips or condiments. By making food from scratch with whole ingredients including fruits, vegetables, nuts, seeds and good oils, you remove the mystery of what you're feeding your body because you know exactly what went into it.

The
Real Food
Kitchen

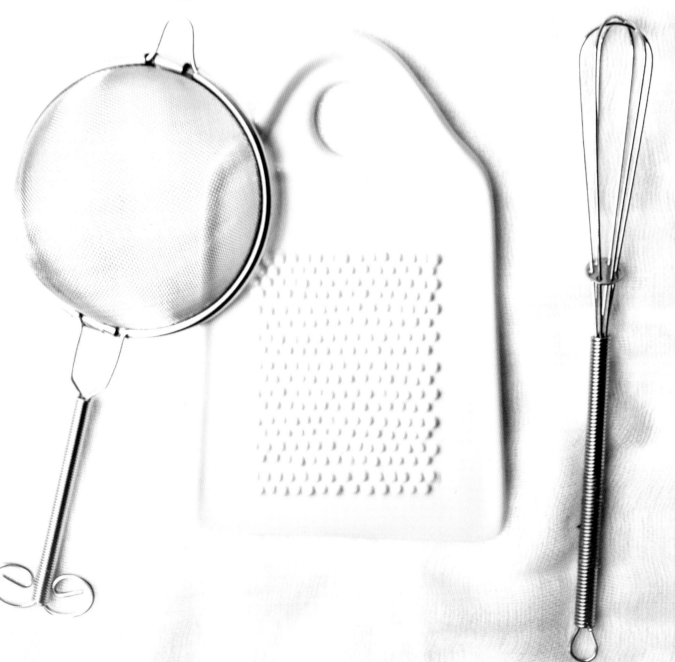

There are many factors that affect the extent to which we can set up our kitchens for good health, including financial and space restrictions. While budgets can influence the ingredients we buy, even the smallest kitchen can be transformed into a healthy environment with a little know-how.

When it comes to kitchen equipment I love a good gadget but have a few staples I use day in day out.

KNIVES

A good set of knives is a must. When you're spending your hard earned money on free range cuts of meat or organic produce, the last thing you want to do is try and cut through them with a blunt knife. Buy the best you can afford and keep them sharp, you'll use them every day.

MEASURING CUPS AND SPOONS

I do have a set of scales in my kitchen but I much prefer to use measuring cups and, after a period of time, to eyeball the measurements as I'm cooking. Weighing can be necessary in certain recipes but my style of cooking is to go with the flow and improvise as need be. Standard measuring spoons that are handy to have are ¼ teaspoon, ½ teaspoon, 1 teaspoon and 1 tablespoon.

WHISK AND SIEVE

A good balloon whisk is an essential, as is a fine mesh sieve. When recipes go awry, these two handy tools always get called in to try and redeem the mixture before it heads to the bin. Is something lumpy when it shouldn't be? Give it a good whisk.

SPATULA

I always have a couple of silicone spatulas on hand, especially when baking to ensure I get every last drop of mixture from the bowl to the baking pan to the oven to my mouth.

FOOD PROCESSOR

This is the Big Kahuna of kitchen equipment that makes your Real Food life that much easier. It's also one piece of equipment that I believe is non negotiable if you want to get serious about real cooking for health. I'm not saying everyone needs to have a full bench top model with all the bells and whistles, I find that a small handheld processor or immersion blender with bowl attachments can work just as well, and can be bought for under $100 (£50). Having a food processor will allow you to make your own nut butters and flours, your own condiments and sauces, fresh made dips, pureed soups, the list goes on.

BLENDER

If you have the space, money and inclination, adding a blender to your kitchen is a wise investment. Having said that, if you have a good quality food processor you can afford to skip the blender if need be. My advice would be to start with the food processor and move up from there. Blenders are great for making smoothies and often produce nut butters much quicker and easier than a food processor.

JUICER

As with the blender, if you have the space, money and inclination, adding a juicer to your kitchen is not essential but can help you create delicious and healthy drinks. I avoid juicing 100% fruit and opt for an 80% vegetables-20% fruit combination. Having a juicer on hand for days when I need an energy boost or need to up my vegetable intake is incredibly handy.

VEGETABLE SPIRALISER

For those wanting to cut down on wheat or those who just love their veg, a spiraliser is a must in your kitchen. Turning vegetables into noodles opens up a whole new world of tasty dishes and textures. Spiralisers range from handheld to compact bench top models and are very affordable. A handheld julienne peeler is a great alternative to a full spiraliser as you can use it to make noodles or to finely slice vegetables for salads.

ZESTER

Adding flavour to a dish couldn't be simpler than zesting a lemon or a chunk of ginger. While you don't necessarily need the most expensive brand, I find that the cheaper ones don't zest as fine and tend not to last as long as those that cost a little extra.

A SENSE OF ADVENTURE

Corny I know, but without a sense of culinary adventure your Real Food journey will be a short one. I open up my mind and palate to the endless possibilities that lie before me each time I visit the farmers' market or step into the kitchen.

Real Food *Staples*

Stocking your Real Food pantry for the first time may strike you as an expensive endeavour, and it can be, however remember the following things:

✳ Buying in bulk can save you money in the long run, especially with dry goods you can store for a couple of months at a time in airtight containers. Find a bulk food source close to home, where nuts, seeds and grains among other similar items are stocked in large bins with a lower price point than your local supermarket. If you can't locate one of these stores look online for a wholesaler or retailer who can ship direct to your door.

✳ If finances are an issue choose one area to focus on first, with the intention to widen your Real Food pantry when you can afford to. You may want to focus first on breakfast, stocking up on ingredients that will allow you to break free from the cereal and toast maze. Alternatively, you may decide to replace the vegetable or seed oil in your cupboard with coconut oil, or switch the white sugar for good quality maple syrup; even a few small changes in the beginning can make a big difference.

✳ Take a moment to consider how you spend your money. What do you deem worthy of parting ways with your cash for? Rent or a mortgage is a given, perhaps your car, entertainment or travel? Where does your health rank on the list? We've become conditioned to think we should pay as little as possible for the food we eat when it should be the opposite. Putting your health first helps the rest of your life follow, putting you in the best position to deal with the highs and lows that come your way.

✳ Organic, free range and grass fed are often considered luxuries. There's certainly ways to improve your lifestyle without buying these 100% of the time, however if you reduced the frequency of eating these ingredients but increased the overall quality then you're not only doing better by the animal during its life but also ensuring optimal nutrition when you consume them. Try substituting one regular meat meal a week with free range and grass fed products and keep going from there. Take a stand to only buy free-range eggs, not only is it the best ethical choice but the eggs taste better too.

✳ Fresh fruits and vegetables should be weekly or bi-weekly purchases, along with seafood and meat if you eat them. Go for seasonal produce to ensure a lower price point and to feed your body the types of food it needs during different times of the year. Shopping at a local farmers' market will help you know what is in season and you can often get a much better deal than you would at the supermarket. We all have our own favourite fruits and vegetables but try to diversify what you buy and add different produce to your basket now and then.

Oils, Milks + Vinegars

APPLE CIDER VINEGAR
This is one of those magic ingredients no kitchen should be without. It earns its weight in gold not only in the kitchen but as a beauty product too. Buy apple cider vinegar (ACV) that contains the "mother" to ensure a premium product, it should be clearly labelled on the bottle. ACV is a great alkalising ingredient and can be used to help combat digestive issues, as a skin toner or hair conditioner, or simply as an alternative to vinegars such as balsamic in dressings and sauces.

COCONUT MILK
My husband often questions why we need so many tins of coconut milk in the cupboard, to me coconut milk is the equivalent to my mother's habit of always having a tin or two of diced tomatoes on hand, just in case. This dairy-free milk always comes in handy when whipping up a breakfast, smoothie, curry, soup or dessert. It never ceases to amaze me how a tin of coconut milk can truly transform a dish from average to creamy heaven. Simply use as you would dairy milk or cream. Store the coconut milk in the fridge overnight to help solidify the milk liquids into cream; you can then whip this as you would dairy cream for desserts.

COCONUT OIL
Much like apple cider vinegar, coconut oil is not only useful in the kitchen but also as a beauty product. Coconut oil is a great skin moisturiser, make up remover, hair conditioner and can even be "pulled" in the mouth to help clean teeth.

In the kitchen coconut oil is great for cooking at high tempera-tures, as it's more stable than olive oil and won't oxidise and create free radicals, and is a much healthier choice than seed or vegetable oils, such as canola or sunflower. Used in desserts, coconut oil can be melted to create raw chocolate and can replace other oils in baked goods.

Coconut milk and oil contain short-term medium-chain fatty acids (MCFAs), which our liver converts into energy not fat. Consuming MCFAs is great muscle and brain fuel.

COCONUT WATER
While not as essential in the kitchen as coconut milk or oil, coconut water is handy to add flavour to smoothies while not changing the consistency of the drink. Boasting high levels of electrolytes, coconut water is a great drink after intense exercise but can easily be replaced with filtered water in recipes. Check the ingredients list to make sure you are buying 100% coconut water with no added sugar or additives.

OLIVE OIL
While olive oil isn't the best choice for high temperature cooking, having a great quality, organic if possible, extra virgin olive oil on hand to add to sauces and dressings or drizzle over salads or vegetables is a must. Go for a mild, light flavoured oil for roasting vegetables in and experiment with flavour strength when choosing one to enjoy "raw".

NUT + OAT MILKS
Making milk, sometimes called mylk, from nuts and oats is a popular option for vegans, lactose intolerant people or those who prefer not to consume dairy. While you can buy almond milk in most supermarkets now, they can be expensive and often contain unnecessary ingredients, including sugar. It's easy to make your own nut and oak milks at home if you have a blender to do the hard work for you. You can drink nut milk straight or use it in recipes that call for dairy milk.

BASIC NUT MILK
MAKES 4 CUPS/1 LITRE

1½ cups (210g) almonds, cashews or Brazil nuts
Water
Optional sweetener such as Medjool dates, maple syrup, rice malt syrup, vanilla powder or cinnamon

Soak the nuts overnight in a bowl of filtered water. Rinse the nuts in fresh water, drain then add to a blender with 4 cups (1L) of filtered water. Blend on high until smooth. Place a sieve over a large bowl or jug. Line the sieve with a piece of muslin cloth and pour the nut milk through the cloth to separate the pulp from the milk. Squeeze the pulp in the cloth to drain as much liquid as possible. The nut pulp can be dehydrated into nut meal, added to smoothies or sent to the compost heap.

If you would like to sweeten the nut milk, blend the sweetener of choice into the strained milk before storing in an airtight jar or container in the fridge. Nut milk is usually good for up to 5 days.

OAT MILK
MAKES 4 CUPS/1 LITRE

1½ cups (120g) rolled oats (not quick oats)
Water
Optional sweetener such as Medjool dates, maple syrup, rice malt syrup, vanilla powder or cinnamon

Soak the oats in a bowl of filtered water for 1 hour before draining through a sieve, rinsing with fresh water and adding to a blender with 4 cups (1L) of filtered water. Blend on high until smooth. Place a sieve over a large bowl or jug. Line the sieve with a piece of muslin cloth and pour the milk through the cloth to separate the pulp from the milk. Squeeze the pulp in the cloth to drain as much liquid as possible. Discard the oat pulp in the compost heap or bin.

If adding a sweetener to the oat milk, blend the strained milk with the sweetener of choice before storing the milk in an airtight container in the fridge.

Sweeteners

RAW HONEY

Raw honey, that is locally sourced and hasn't been heat-treated, has an abundance of healing properties to consider. You won't find this type of honey on your supermarket shelf, anything sitting there has been heat treated and processed to remove all of the beneficial elements and leave only the sweetness. Your local farmers' market is a great source for raw honey, as is the Internet. It's amazing what you can source online these days; with many metropolitan areas boasting rooftop honey schemes ensuring local bees and minimal human interference. Raw honey ensures a premium product that has retained most or all of the beneficial enzymes, natural vitamins and antioxidants. It is anti viral, anti bacterial, promotes good digestive health and can be a powerful aid in treating allergies, particularly hay fever. A little bit goes a long way so you'll find a jar of raw honey can keep you going for many months, if not longer. If you can't source good quality raw honey don't substitute with a supermarket shelf brand, simply avoid it entirely.

MAPLE SYRUP

As with honey, maple syrup comes in myriad of qualities and the more you pay, the purer the product will be. It is incredibly sweet so only a small amount goes a long way in recipes; I'm not suggesting dousing a stack of pancakes in the stuff, as it is traditionally used for. Its health benefits include a high level of manganese, which is great for energy and in strengthening your immunity, and high levels of zinc, also good for the immune system and for reproductive health. Look for organic Grade A pure maple syrup and avoid maple "flavoured" syrup, which is a highly refined product lacking the benefits of the pure product.

RICE MALT SYRUP

Rice malt syrup is fructose free and is made from brown rice using a process where the rice is cultured with enzymes to break down the starch; it's then cooked until it becomes a syrup. Rice malt syrup is a complex carbohydrate with maltose (malt sugar) and a small amount of glucose. It can usually be found in the health food aisle of most supermarkets, in health stores or online. It is relatively cheap and a little tends to go a long way but being a liquid is not as easy to substitute in recipes calling for white sugar and may take some experimenting to perfect. Rice malt syrup is a great option because of its low cost, ease of use and taste but it should still be used in moderation and not become an everyday product. When buying, look for a brand with 100% rice in the ingredients list, anything more and the product is not pure.

MEDJOOL DATES

On the whole, dates and other dried fruits should be consumed sparingly. The dehydration process concentrates the fruit's natural fructose as water is removed and the fruit shrinks in size, often meaning you end up eating a larger quantity. However, when used in desserts or sweet treats sparingly, especially when shared with friends and family, including dates boats some health benefits in addition to their great taste. They are high in magnesium and zinc, and full of fibre, just remember to consume them in moderation. I opt for Medjool dates over other varieties as they are softer and blend much better. Soaking the dates in hot water before blending will also help create a smooth date paste.

Nuts, Seeds + Flours

PEPITAS

Pepitas (pumpkin seeds) are a nutritional powerhouse and are great to keep on hand in your pantry to top homemade muffins, soups and granola, or added to smoothies. Rich in magnesium, zinc and a great source of protein, pepitas are great immunity boosters and can help with insulin regulation, great for people with diabetes, or to balance out a sweeter ingredient, such as dates. Pepitas can be roasted with spices, ground into a paste or dip, or enjoyed raw.

SUNFLOWER SEEDS

Sunflower seeds are a heart healthy snack rich in vitamin E, selenium and magnesium. The high level of vitamin E is particularly beneficial as it can help reduce inflammation in the body and ease the symptoms of arthritis, joint pain and asthma. Sprinkle sunflower seeds over your morning porridge or acai bowl, add to a smoothie or stir through a salad.

CHIA SEEDS

This native South American crop is a great source of sustained energy to add to your meals. The seeds are packed full of calcium, magnesium, fibre, Omega 3s, manganese and phosphorus. The high level of antioxidants in chia seeds stops the crop from going rancid and a small amount in your diet each day or two goes a long way. Try eating raw; sprinkled over salads, added to smoothies, acai bowls, in baked goods or in the chia pudding recipe on page 33.

BUCKWHEAT

Despite its name, buckwheat is not in fact a wheat product. The proteins in this fruit seed are highly digestive and readily available to your body; it is a great gluten free alternative to wheat cereals and a great option for those on a grain free diet. You can use buckwheat whole, as you would rice or quinoa; as a flour in baked goods, puffed in cereals, or buy premade buckinis, where the buckwheat has been soaked, washed, rinsed and then dehydrated at low temperatures to create a crunchy treat.

QUINOA

Another great gluten and wheat free option, this complete protein can easily be substituted in recipes calling for rice and is a great source of calcium, magnesium and manganese. It's important to thoroughly rinse the quinoa prior to cooking to remove the natural bitterness, then simply cook using the absorption method you would use for rice. Quinoa is quite bland in flavour so is a great blank canvas to add spices and herbs to, it can easily be added to salads, soups and curries, or provide a surprising texture in desserts – see the crispy caramel cups on page 149.

COCONUT FLOUR

Coconut flour is a great grain free option for baking, although it's not as simple as a 1:1 replacement for refined white flour. Coconut flour is more absorbent than white flour and requires the addition of a larger amount of eggs or fluid to the recipe to achieve a palatable texture in the finished product. The general rule seems to be, use ¼ cup of coconut flour for each cup of wheat flour in a recipe and adding 1 egg for every 30g/1 oz of flour used. Coconut flour is a more expensive option when substituting for white flour, and can take some practice to perfect in recipes. If you're interested in utilising this ingredient try following a few tried and tested recipes (which you can easily source online) first so you learn how it behaves.

RICE FLOUR

This gluten free flour is prepared by grinding the broken rice grain during milling and can be purchased in white and brown varieties. Rice flour is a much easier substitute for wheat flour than coconut flour is, and can be used in a 1:1 ratio. Rice flour is a good source of fibre, selenium, magnesium and phosphorus, and is a neutral flavoured flour that can be used in sweet or savoury dishes. Purchase in the health food aisle of the supermarket or health food stores and store in an airtight container in the cupboard.

CHICKPEA FLOUR

Chickpea flour, also known as Besan or gram flour, is a great gluten free flour alternative that is high in iron, folate, protein and fibre. Made from ground up raw or roasted chickpeas, this subtle-tasting, nutty flour is a versatile kitchen staple in many cultures. In addition to using chickpea flour in baking, it can be used to thicken sauces and soups, or mixed with spices, oil and water to create a flatbread (see page 98) or used to bind fritters. Try mixing chickpea and rice flours in a 1:1 ratio.

VANILLA POWDER

When buying vanilla powder make sure it is pure and contains no other ingredients, such as sugar, which is often added to bulk the vanilla up. Vanilla powder is a great alternative to vanilla extract and even to vanilla pods, which can get expensive when using in a lot of cooking. With a lingering flavour, the powder is easy to add to baked goods and smoothies. While buying initially will incur a slight expense compared to the cheaper vanilla essences and even extracts, a little bit of vanilla powder goes a long way, so it will last you a good 4–6 months.

RAW CACAO POWDER

When a recipe calls for raw cacao powder it doesn't mean cocoa powder, which is a more refined version easily found on the super-market shelf. Raw cacao is starting to creep into supermarkets but is more readily available at health food or specialty grocers. Raw cacao is made by cold-pressing raw, unroasted cocoa beans, while cocoa powder is the result of roasting the beans, which retains the chocolate flavour but removes the beneficial enzymes. Raw cacao powder is a more expensive option than cocoa powder but boasts many health benefits including lowering insulin resistance, reducing blood pressure, and boosting your mood thanks to the high levels of magnesium. Plus it tastes delicious too, adding a chocolate flavour to smoothies, breakfast bowls and desserts.

ALMOND MEAL

Almond meal is made from finely ground almonds with the skins on, while almond flour is usually made from blanched almonds with no skin. While almond flour will give you a finer texture in a baked good, I find almond meal more readily available at the supermarket and don't mind the coarser texture. You can also make your own almond meal at home with the help of a high-powered food pro-cessor, and can even dehydrate the leftover almonds after making nut milk (see page 13) to turn into meal. I bake with almond or nut meals with caution as the amount consumed is more than you would consume having a handful of nuts so it is an occasional ingredient rather than a daily one.

ALMONDS, CASHEWS + HAZELNUTS

The main nuts used in the follow-ing recipes are almonds, cashews and hazelnuts. Peanuts are generally avoided as they are the most vulnerable nut to go rancid and can easily be replaced with other nuts without compromising taste or texture. Nuts are easier to use if they have been soaked overnight in filtered water and rinsed; this not only makes them easier to blend but also removes the enzyme inhibitors, phytic acid, polyphenols and goitrogens that coat the nuts. While the above are useful to the plant in nature, to help it survive until the right growing conditions are present, they're not so helpful to our gut and digestion. When used in moderation, nuts are an extremely beneficial and versatile ingredient, adding taste and texture to any meal of the day, from breakfast granola to a crunchy soup topping, or a baked treat.

SHREDDED COCONUT

As with coconut milk and oil, shredded coconut is a must-have ingredient for adding flavour, natural sweetness, and texture to a dish. Look for unsweetened shredded or desiccated coconut with no anti-caking agents. It can be hard to find such a pure product in the regular supermarket so you may need to venture to a health food store or specialty grocer.

GOJI BERRIES

These chewy morsels of goodness contain the highest concentration of protein of any fruit, contain all the essential amino acids, and are loaded with vitamin C. Surprisingly, goji berries contain 15 times more iron than spinach, as well as containing a host of minerals including calcium, zinc and selenium. While an expensive addition to your kitchen cupboard, they're not an everyday item and a small amount adds sweetness to breakfast bowls or desserts. You can mix a handful of goji berries with some nuts for an on-the-go snack or soak the berries in water to soften then add to your smoothie.

Eating seasonally + *locally*

The shift from eating seasonally and locally to eating whatever was made available to us in a supermarket was swift. It's hard to deny the convenience of our modern way of shopping and eating. Most people in the Western world now have immediate access to a wide range of fresh and cooked food from many countries and cultures; it's both a blessing and curse that our palates are so diverse.

If you stopped to ask someone in the street whether they knew what vegetables were in season in May, or which fruits they should enjoy in February before they're on their way out in March, you'd be hard pressed to find a majority who would be able to answer. We've become disconnected from what we eat, unfamiliar with the farm to table process, uninterested in who grows our food, when it is grown and when it should be eaten.

The first step to getting back to basics is visiting your local farmers' market. If you don't have a market close to you, head online to research farm to customer schemes in your area, there are many companies that will deliver a box of seasonal produce to your door each week. If you're fortunate enough to have a local market, wait until you've visited to see what's available for purchase before planning your meals for the weekend or week.

Often we are drawn to cook certain recipes or cuisines based on the plethora of cooking shows, magazines, books and blogs that are available to us now. While there is definite merit in gaining some culinary inspiration now and then, it's even better if you can adapt those recipes you crave to include ingredients in season.

By buying produce at your local farmers' market you're also ensuring you're buying local and can talk to the grower of your food. Is the stock grass fed? How has the season been, is it better to buy X, Y or Z? How do you cook this produce at home? You'll get much more information and ideas from them than you would a sales assistant at the local super-market. You're also supporting the farmer's livelihood and your local community, even if you only do part of your weekly shop with them.

There are of course undeniable financial benefits to eating seasonally, as any fig lover will testify. Each year fig season begins and ends just as quickly, with a small window of afford-able fruit the price quickly escalates as the short season comes to a close. There are other examples of course, many produce items that stick around our shelves much longer than figs but have an equal price fluctuation. Buying at the peak of production means

more produce in your basket for less, and often better tasting produce at its ripest. Buy extra produce while in season, especially berries and fruit, and freeze in portions for the end of the season when prices may inflate.

The best thing about eating seasonally is the diversity it injects into your diet and cooking. You may go out looking for one ingredient and are forced to use another, making you rethink your dinner plans and get creative. It also prompts you to eat fruits and vegetables you may often shun in favour of more staple ingredients like apples and potatoes. While most people do stick to berries in the summer and warming winter vegetables like pumpkin in the cooler months, we also hang on to certain produce longer than we probably should, especially with frozen fruit available year-round.

The list of what's in season will vary between countries and hemispheres so it's best to search online for a list that correlates with where you live. It's handy to print or write the list out each month to have with you when you go shopping or to reference when planning your meals.

While eating seasonally is ideal, there's always a little room for compromise, especially when wanting to try a new recipe or really craving something, like a berry crumble in winter. If you do all of your food shopping at a supermarket, why not venture out to a farmers' market for the produce, and stick to the store for your staples? The idea is to try new things, get in touch with your food and its supplier, and above all have fun discovering the tastes and textures of the different seasons.

Build your menu around what's in season to enjoy the produce at its ripest + save money. Buy extra when on special + freeze in portions for the end of the season when prices may fluctuate.

WAXED
PINK
LADY
$2.00
KILO

WAXED
FUJI
$2.00
KILO

Discover
the tastes +
textures of
the seasons

ORGANIC –
IS IT WORTH IT?

Eating organic food isn't achievable for a lot of people; there simply isn't the money in the budget to stretch that far. While excessive exposure to toxic pesticides often used to spray our fruits and vegetables has been suggested to cause ailments including hormone disruption, the fact that regularly grown produce is a fraction of the cost of organic is enough to sway most consumers. If you can afford to buy some or all organic produce and meat it's a real investment in your health. If you'd like to try introducing a few organic products and seeing how your budget fares, try following the Dirty Dozen and Clean 15 lists. Real change takes time and must be sustainable, work out what suits you, your budget and your family the best.

THE DIRTY DOZEN –
BUY ORGANIC IF YOU CAN

* Apples
* Celery
* Sweet bell peppers
* Peaches
* Strawberries
* Nectarines
* Grapes
* Spinach
* Lettuce
* Cucumbers
* Blueberries
* Potatoes

THE CLEAN 15 –
LEAST CONTAMINATED BY PESTICIDES

* Onions
* Sweet corn
* Pineapples
* Avocado
* Cabbage
* Sweet peas
* Asparagus
* Mangoes
* Eggplant/Aubergine
* Kiwi
* Cantaloupe
* Sweet potatoes
* Grapefruit
* Watermelon
* Mushrooms

Rise
AND
Shine

BRUNCH SALAD

Despite being called a brunch salad, this can be eaten at any time of the day. You can substitute any leafy green for the kale (such as spinach) and interchange your protein (exchange chicken for canned tuna or leftover roast meat from last night's dinner); there are no rules, use what you love or simply what's in your refrigerator.

SERVES 2-4

1 medium bunch (approximately 450g/1 lb) of kale, stems removed
3 tomatoes
1 lemon
4 free range eggs
250g/9 oz chicken breast fillet, thinly sliced
1 avocado

LEMON DILL SAUCE

2 tbsp extra virgin olive oil
2 tbsp fresh lemon juice
1 tbsp fresh dill, finely chopped
Sea salt and black pepper to taste

Pre-heat the oven to 180°C/350°F. Thickly slice the tomatoes and lemon into rounds and lay on an oven tray lined with baking paper. Spray with olive or coconut oil and season with salt and pepper. Roast in the oven for 20 minutes, remove and let cool.

Prepare the lemon dill sauce by whisking all ingredients together in a bowl or jug.

Cut the kale leaves into chunks and transfer to a small bowl. Pour over half the lemon dill sauce and use your hands to massage the sauce into the leaves until tender. If you are using baby kale, simply pour the sauce over the leaves and gently toss.

Place the eggs in a small saucepan and cover with cold water. Bring to the boil and cook to your liking (2 minutes for a soft boiled egg, 4-5 minutes for medium boiled, depending on the size of the eggs). Once the eggs have cooled, peel the shell off. Alternatively, poach the eggs in a saucepan of simmering water for runny yolks.

Slice the chicken breast into thin strips and heat up a small pan. Season the chicken with a pinch of black pepper. Add a drizzle of extra virgin olive oil to the pan and cook the chicken for 5 minutes, cutting into a strip to check it is cooked through before removing all chicken from the pan and setting aside. Alternatively, use leftover roast chicken that has been shredded.

Slice the avocado to desired thickness and drizzle fresh lemon juice over the top.

Assemble the salad starting with the kale, adding the avocado, eggs, roasted tomato, chicken and finishing with the remaining lemon dill sauce and roasted lemon.

WOK EGGS WITH FRESH GREENS

Breakfast can be simple, speedy and nutritious with a little forward thinking. By cooking the eggs in the wok they are ready to eat in under a minute. Preparing the greens the night before and simply dressing before you eat is another way to ensure you make a healthier choice when pushed for time.

SERVES 2

4 free range eggs
2 spring onions/scallions, roughly chopped
Pinch of sea salt
A mix of watercress, baby spinach and rocket (arugula) leaves, rinsed and dried
1 avocado
¼ cup (60ml) extra virgin olive oil
¼ cup (60ml) fresh lemon juice
1 tbsp good quality seeded mustard

Heat a wok with 1 tbsp of coconut oil, swirl the oil around to coat halfway up the sides. Toss a few sea salt granules into the wok to see if it is hot enough, they should sizzle.

Crack the eggs into a bowl and give them a quick whisk before pouring into the wok. Working quickly, use a silicone spatula to move around the outside of the egg mixture, ensuring it doesn't stick to the wok. After 20 seconds, fold the egg mixture in half, as you would for an omelette. Loosen the bottom of themixture and continue cooking for another 20-30 seconds before removing from the wok and setting aside.

Add the rinsed greens to a bowl with the sliced avocado. In a small bowl or jug whisk the extra virgin olive oil, lemon juice and mustard together before pouring over the greens. Serve the eggs alongside the greens and avocado.

SWEET POTATO + BACON MINI LOAVES

Navigating a low sugar breakfast can be difficult when you first start eating Real Food, especially when you want a slice of bread in the morning but you don't want to lather it in jam or other condiments. Try this savoury sweet potato and bacon loaf that's delicious hot or cold, and gives you a head start on hitting your daily vegetable quota. Serve with a smear of butter or try something different, such as ricotta or smashed avocado.

SERVES 2

½ cup (65g) brown rice flour
½ cup (50g) almond meal/flour
½ tsp baking soda
2 tsp ground cinnamon
3 free range eggs
½ cup (125ml) coconut oil, melted
¼ cup (60ml) rice malt syrup (optional)
1 medium sweet potato
1 small zucchini/courgette
1 tsp sea salt
½ tsp black pepper
2 bacon rashers, any cut

Preheat the oven to 180°C/350°F.

Sift flours, baking powder and cinnamon into a bowl, set aside.

Whisk eggs, coconut oil and rice malt syrup together and fold through the dry mixture.

Grate the sweet potato and zucchini, season with salt and pepper and add to the mixture. Add a little more coconut oil if the mixture is too dry.

Divide the batter between two mini loaf pans. Alternatively, use one larger loaf pan and increase the cooking time.

Dice bacon and sprinkle evenly over the top of each loaf.

Bake in the oven for 50-60 minutes. The loaves are cooked through when an inserted skewer comes out clean.

SPROUTED LENTIL + ARTICHOKE BOWL

This salad makes a refreshing change from the typical idea of what breakfast can be. If you're not keen on sprouting your own lentils right away, you can buy them from specialty produce stores and some supermarkets. Top the bowl with a cooked egg for a protein boost.

SERVES 1

Sprouted lentils
2 cups (400g) dried lentils of choice
Glass jar
Muslin or breathable cloth to cover
   the jar

Prepare the sprouted lentils ahead of time by soaking them in filtered water overnight, or for up to 14 hours. Rinse the lentils thoroughly and drain any excess liquid. Place the lentils in a glass jar and cover the top with muslin cloth, secure with a rubber band. Store the jar on the kitchen counter and rinse the lentils once a day in water, making sure to drain any water before returning the lentils to the jar.

   The lentils should begin sprouting after 3 days. Test one is ready before rinsing the lentils for the final time. Return the lentils to the jar, secure the cloth on top and store in the refrigerator for up to two weeks. If the lentils are slimy or smell off-putting, bin the batch and start again.

ARTICHOKE BOWL

1 cup (200g) sprouted lentils
½ cup (100g) artichoke hearts
   (store-bought in brine is fine)
1 inch piece of fresh ginger, grated
Juice and zest of ½ a lemon
Pinch of sea salt and black pepper
1 free range egg (optional)

In a small bowl combine lentils, artichokes, fresh ginger, lemon juice and zest. Stir, taste and adjust seasoning with sea salt and black pepper.
   Cook egg to your liking (if using) and serve on top of the salad.

STRAWBERRY CHIA PUDDING

This make-ahead breakfast is refreshing in the warmer months when seasonal fruit is at its ripest. Berries work great here or you could stew some stone fruit or apples in cinnamon then mix through the milk and chia seeds for a different flavour and texture.

SERVES 1

1 cup (250ml) coconut milk, full fat milk or any nut milk
1 cup (130g) fresh or frozen strawberries
½ cup (80g) shredded coconut
1 tbsp rice malt syrup or sweetener of choice
½ tsp vanilla powder
1 tsp cinnamon
2 tbsp chia seeds

In a blender or with a handheld immersion blender, puree milk, strawberries, shredded coconut, rice malt syrup and vanilla powder. Transfer the mixture to a bowl and whisk in the cinnamon and chia seeds. Place in the refrigerator for one hour to set. Serve at room temperature or chilled, topped with extra coconut and strawberries if desired.

ZESTY CITRUS GRANOLA

A tasty alternative to store-bought cereal or granola, making it yourself allows you to control the flavour and amount of sweetener added. This zingy combination of lemon and grapefruit zest and juice is complimented by the spiciness of nutmeg and ginger, making it a warming start to the day. Serve with a poached fruit of choice.

SERVES 1

1 cup (100g) quinoa flakes, puffed rice or buckwheat
¼ cup (20g) shredded coconut
2 tbsp coconut oil
1 tbsp rice malt syrup or sweetener of choice
Zest of 1 lemon
Zest of 1 grapefruit
Zest of 1 orange
1 tbsp lemon juice
1 tsp ground nutmeg
1 tsp ground ginger
1 tsp ground cinnamon

Preheat the oven to 180°C/350°F and line an oven tray with baking paper.

Combine the quinoa flakes, shredded coconut, coconut oil, rice malt syrup, lemon, grapefruit and orange zests and juice, ground nutmeg, ginger and cinnamon in a bowl. Spread the mixture evenly over the lined tray and bake in the oven for 10-15 minutes or until golden brown, careful not to let it burn. Remove from the oven, let cool and store in an airtight container.

Serve the granola with milk of choice or natural yoghurt, topped with poached fruit and a sprinkling of lemon zest.

Make granola clusters by mixing everything together with an additional tablespoon of honey or rice malt syrup for added stickiness. Take spoonfuls of the mixture and form into small balls or clumps, evenly space them on an oven tray lined with baking paper and bake until crisp.

PUMPKIN PECAN PIE BREAKFAST BOWL

This recipe truly is like having dessert for breakfast, with the warming and sweet pureed pumpkin paired with the maple roasted pecans and the frothy coconut cream, this is deconstructed pie at its best and healthiest.

SERVES 1

MAPLE ROASTED NUTS
⅓ cup (40g) pecans
1 tbsp maple syrup
¼ tsp ground cinnamon

FROTHY COCONUT CREAM
1 cup (250ml) coconut milk or cream, chilled in the refrigerator overnight
½ tsp vanilla powder

PUMPKIN PIE
250g/9 oz pumpkin, any variety
1 tbsp coconut oil
½ tsp ground cinnamon
½ tsp ground nutmeg

Preheat the oven to 160°C/320°F and line an oven tray with baking paper. Scatter the pecans over the tray and pour the maple syrup and cinnamon over the top. Roast in the oven for 5-10 minutes until browned. Set aside.

To make the coconut cream, pour the coconut milk or cream and the vanilla powder into a bowl and whisk for 5-10 minutes until frothy and thickened. The coconut milk must be chilled for this to work.

Remove the skin from the pumpkin and chop into even chunks. Steam the pumpkin until tender, either using a microwave or in a steamer basket over simmering water. Add the coconut oil, cinnamon and nutmeg to the pumpkin and puree using a blender or handheld immersion blender.

Add the pumpkin puree, frothy coconut cream and pecans to a bowl and enjoy. You can serve the pecans whole or crush them up into a crumble before sprinkling over the top. This can be enjoyed warm or chilled.

ROASTED PLUMS + RICOTTA ON RYE

This is a great make-ahead meal idea that delivers a sweet breakfast in minimal time. Roast the plums the night before and let them soak in their juices before topping your fresh rye bread in the morning. You can replace the plums with any stone fruit or use fresh berries. In the cooler months try substituting with stewed apples or pears.

SERVES 2

4 plums, any variety
1 tsp vanilla powder
½ tsp ground cinnamon
2 slices of dark rye bread
½ cup (130g) smooth ricotta

Preheat the oven to 180°C/350°F. Halve the plums, discarding the stones, and place in a shallow baking dish with the vanilla powder and cinnamon. Bake the plums for 20 minutes or until they are tender and sitting in their own juices.

Spread each slice of rye bread, toasted or fresh, with the ricotta and top with the roasted plums, drizzling extra plum juice over the top. Store any leftover plums in an airtight container in the fridge.

BAKED APPLE + RICOTTA PANCAKES

Pancakes make a great weekend treat but traditional recipes can be heavy on the refined flour and sugar. The beauty of these baked pancakes is the cake-like texture they take on, rather than the thin, often dry texture of many healthy alternatives. Cinnamon apples and ricotta are a great combination but you could also use berries stirred through the mixture for a sweet burst.

MAKES 6

2 large green apples
1 tsp ground cinnamon
½ cup (125ml) filtered water

1 cup (130g) rice flour
1 cup (120g) buckwheat flour
2 tsp baking powder
Pinch of sea salt
3 tbsp maple or rice malt syrup
½ cup (125ml) coconut oil, melted
2 free range eggs
1 cup (250ml) almond milk
150g/5 oz smooth ricotta

Preheat the oven to 180°C/350°F.

Peel and core the apples before dicing into even cubes and placing in a saucepan with the ground cinnamon and water. Stew over a low heat until the apples are tender, about 10 minutes. Set aside to cool.

In a large bowl sift the two flours, baking powder and sea salt. Make a well in the centre and add the maple syrup, melted coconut oil, eggs and almond milk, stir to combine. Fold through the ricotta and the stewed apples until just combined.

Melt a couple of tablespoons of coconut oil in a cast iron pan or oven and stovetop proof dish. Place as many egg rings as you can fit into the pan – if the egg rings are not non-stick then be sure to grease them thoroughly. Pour the batter into each of the egg rings, careful not to fill over half way. Over a medium heat begin cooking the pancakes for 1-2 minutes then transfer to the oven and cook for a further 5 minutes.

Remove the pan from the oven, flip the pancakes to briefly cook the other side, about 2 minutes, and then set aside to cool for a minute before gently removing them from the egg rings.

Serve the pancakes warm with a drizzle of maple syrup, extra stewed apple, chopped nuts or whatever takes your fancy on top.

LEMON + CINNAMON COTTAGE CHEESE PIKELETS

MAKES 12

2 cups (260g) brown rice flour
1 tsp baking powder
½ tsp sea salt
Zest of 1 lemon
1½ tsp ground cinnamon
1 free range egg, whisked
1 cup (250ml) milk
2 tbsp honey or sweetener of choice
½ cup (110g) cottage cheese
1 tbsp lemon juice
Coconut oil for cooking

Sift the flour and baking powder together in a bowl then stir through the salt, lemon zest and cinnamon. Make a well in the centre and add the egg, milk and honey, stir to combine. Stir through the cottage cheese and lemon juice.

Add a couple of tablespoons of coconut oil to a pan and when hot, drop spoonfuls of the mixture in. Wait until bubbles appear over the surface, flip the pikelets and cook for a couple of minutes on the other side. Keep the pikelets small rather than make a large pancake and serve in a stack with fresh lemon juice drizzled over them while warm. Serve with fresh fruit.

These pikelets are a savoury alternative to regular pancakes and contain a minimal amount of sweetener. Pairing the pikelets with fresh fruit will deliver the sweetness you may crave, and substituting more savoury meals into your breakfast routine will help wean you off sweeter starts to the day.

TURMERIC BACON + EGG MUFFINS

These are handy to make and have ready to go in the fridge or enjoyed straight out of the oven. You can add vegetables to the cups or play around with different spices depending on what you have in your cupboard. A word of caution if you have never cooked with turmeric before; it has a potent yellow colour that will stain anything that comes into contact with it, such as bench tops, utensils, skin or clothing. Be careful when cooking with it and if a spill occurs, clean it up immediately.

MAKES 6

6 bacon rashers, any cut
8 free range eggs
4 spring onions/scallions, roughly
  chopped
Sea salt and black pepper
1½ tsp ground turmeric

Preheat the oven to 180°C/350°F.
    Place six muffin liners into the holes of a muffin tray and lay one bacon rasher into each by wrapping it around the inside of the liner.
    Cook the bacon for 10-15 minutes to begin crisping it up. It doesn't matter if the bacon doesn't hold its shape at this point.
    Whisk the eggs until just combined then add spring onions and a pinch of sea salt and black pepper for seasoning. Pour the egg mixture evenly into the 6 muffin liners and sprinkle the top of each with turmeric.
    Cook the bacon and egg muffins in the oven for a further 10 minutes or until the egg is cooked to your liking.

Turmeric is a powerhouse spice that often gets overlooked thanks to its unfortunate ability to stain anything it comes into contact with. Its bright yellow hue is a good signifier of how potent its benefits are and should be cause for you to begin adding more of it to your food. Turmeric is a strong antioxidant and anti-inflammatory and can help prevent insulin resistance. The root plant has long been used in traditional Chinese medicine as a powerful detoxification tool, and is great for repairing the liver. Use ground turmeric found readily in supermarkets, or the root plant, found in some supermarkets or in specialty grocers, produce stores and farmers' markets. If a spill does occur, clean it up immediately with a little bicarb soda and water.

POTATO + LEEK HASH BROWNS

These baked hash browns are a real crowd pleaser, don't require too much prep work and can be topped with an endless array of ingredients. Make a batch ahead of time and freeze in individual portions then simply reheat in the oven for a crispy coating.

MAKES 8

4 medium potatoes
1 leek
25g/1 oz butter
½ cup (65g) rice flour
Sea salt and black pepper

CORIANDER GUACAMOLE
1 large avocado
Juice of ½ a lemon
Handful of coriander/cilantro leaves
Pinch of sea salt

Preheat the oven to 180°C/350°F and line an oven tray with baking paper. Peel the potatoes and cut each into even cubes. Steam the potatoes for 4-5 minutes, either in a microwave or in a steamer basket on the stovetop over simmering water. The potato should be tender but still hold its shape. Take half the mixture and puree it then stir through the rest of the potato so you have a mixture of smooth and chunky potato.
    Clean the leek and dice into even chunks. In a small pan, cook the leek in butter until soft. Set aside to cool slightly then stir through the potato mixture with the rice flour and a good pinch of sea salt and black pepper for flavour.
    Using an egg ring placed on the oven tray as a guide, spoon the mixture into the egg ring and push down until flat. Remove the egg ring carefully, reposition it further along the tray and repeat the process until you have used up all of the mixture. Bake in the oven for 30 minutes or until golden brown.
    Prepare the guacamole by blitzing the avocado, lemon juice, coriander and sea salt in a food processor until smooth. Serve the guacamole on top of the hash browns along with any additional toppings such as roasted cherry tomatoes.

Acai bowls

These tasty bowls of fruity goodness have been growing in popularity in recent years. Often turning into elaborate works of art worthy of an Instagram post, they can be on the more expensive side of breakfast options because of the acai berry, a native of Brazil, and the various toppings used. An acai bowl is the closest you can come to eating a bowl of ice cream for breakfast without feeling remorse.

Build your own bowl

There really are no rules when it comes to an acai bowl, the more ingredients the merrier! Customise to your taste, region and season with a delicious combination of nuts, seeds and fruits. Start with the base recipe below and try some of the suggested combinations. Acai berries can be found as a frozen puree at health stores or specialty grocers

BASE RECIPE

1 large banana, frozen
1 acai berry puree pack
½-1 cup (125-250ml) milk of choice or water, depending on desired thickness

Peel the banana and slice into even chunks ahead of time. Freeze in ziplock bags for easy access. When ready to build your acai bowl base, remove the acai puree pack from the freezer and run under warm water for 15-20 seconds to help soften it slightly. Run it under the water too long and you risk melting it, which will affect the final texture of the bowl.

Add the frozen banana, acai berry puree and milk of choice (dairy, oat, almond, coconut) to a blender or the bowl of a food processor. Blitz on high to desired consistency, adding more liquid if needed.

CHOC-BEET

Replace the frozen banana in the base recipe with one cooked beetroot, peeled and diced into even chunks.

Blitz the beetroot, ⅓ cup (30g) of raw cacao powder, the acai berry puree and milk of choice until smooth and creamy. Top with chocolate buckinis (page 65).

SPINACH KIWI CRUSH

Blitz the base acai bowl recipe with 2 cups (60g) of baby spinach leaves and an additional ½ cup (125ml) of your milk of choice. Top the acai bowl with thin slices of kiwi fruit and crushed walnuts for added texture.

SWEET POTATO + COCONUT

Remove the skin then steam a medium sized sweet potato. Puree using a food processor or stick blender and set aside to cool. Blitz the sweet potato puree with the acai puree pack and 1 cup (250ml) of coconut milk. Toast 1 cup (80g) of unsweetened shredded coconut in a dry pan, careful not to let it burn, and sprinkle over the top of the acai bowl with a handful of pepitas/pumpkin seeds.

ALMOND GRANOLA JOY

Use the base acai bowl recipe and blend using almond milk. Top the acai bowl with the following granola recipe. Preheat the oven to 160°C/320°F and line an oven tray with baking paper. In a bowl combine 1 cup (100g) of quinoa flakes with 1 cup (170g) of roughly chopped almonds, ½ cup (40g) of unsweetened shredded coconut, 1 tsp ground cinnamon and ⅓ cup (80ml) rice malt syrup. Spread the mixture over the tray and bake in the oven for 25 minutes or until the mixture has crisped up. Remove from the oven, let cool for 10 minutes then break into chunks with your hands. Store any unused granola in an airtight container for up to a week.

CACAO + AVOCADO

Replace the frozen banana in the base acai bowl recipe with ½ an avocado and blitz with 2 tbsp raw cacao powder. Top the bowl with the chocolate buckinis (page 65) and fresh berries for extra sweetness.

BLUEBERRY + YOGHURT

Blitz the base acai bowl recipe with ½ cup (125ml) milk of choice and ½ cup (135g) of natural unsweetened yoghurt. For the topping, bake 1 cup (150g) of blueberries in the oven for 15 minutes at 180°C/350°F, until the juices begin seeping out. Stir the baked blueberries through ½ cup (135g) of natural unsweetened yoghurt and drizzle over the top of the acai bowl. Place ½ cup (70g) of sunflower seeds in the bowl of a food processor with ½ tsp of vanilla powder, or use a mortar and pestle, and blitz until a crumb forms, sprinkle over the top of the bowl.

Beetroots
with Leaves
$5.00
bunch

Loose Beetroots
$2.99 $
kg.

CUCUMBER CHIA SMOOTHIE

Cucumber is a fantastic hydrating ingredient to add to smoothies and juices. Combine cucumber in this smoothie with an apple for sweetness and chia seeds for fibre and protein, and you have a delicious and energising drink to kick start your day or boost your energy in the afternoon.

SERVES 2

1 tbsp chia seeds
½ cup (125ml) filtered water
1 cucumber, any variety, diced
1 cup (30g) green leaves of choice
½ an apple
1 tbsp nut butter (optional)
2 cups (500ml) milk of choice

Soak the chia seeds in the water for 15 minutes then add to a blender with the cucumber, green leaves, apple, nut butter and milk, blend on high until smooth.

CHOC MALT CACAO NIB CRUNCH

This healthy spin on the classic chocolate milkshake is a treasure trove of flavour thanks to a combination of cacao, vanilla and maca root powder. While maca can be omitted from the recipe, this ground root is rich in B vitamins as well as vitamins C and E. It's also a great hormone balancing ingredient rich in iron, zinc and magnesium.

SERVES 1

1 banana, frozen
1½ cups (375ml) coconut milk
1½ tbsp maca root powder
1 tbsp raw cacao powder
½ tsp vanilla powder
1 tbsp cacao nibs, to serve

Add the banana, coconut milk, maca root, cacao and vanilla powders to a blender and blitz on high until combined. Pour into a tall glass and serve with cacao nibs sprinkled on top.

COCONUT + CUCUMBER LEMONADE

This refreshing drink can be made as a juice or blended into a smoothie, depending on your preference. Add a small knob of fresh ginger root for an added bite and serve with plenty of ice and fresh mint sprigs.

SERVES 2

1 large cucumber
1 cup (160g) pineapple chunks, freeze the fruit if making a smoothie
Juice from 1 lemon
2 cups (500ml) coconut water

Juice the cucumber and pineapple in your juicer then add the lemon juice and coconut water to the jug and stir to thoroughly combine.

If making a smoothie, dice the cucumber into similar-sized chunks and add to the blender with the pineapple, lemon juice and coconut water. Blitz until smooth. You can replace the coconut water with coconut milk for an even creamier treat.

LIME, GINGER + CELERY BOOSTER

This is a great morning drink to wake up and cleanse your system. Only juice the lime peel if you are using organic produce, otherwise peel the lime and juice the flesh only. If it's a larger lime then use only half of the peel in your juice, you can zest the remaining half and add to water in an ice cube tray to use at a later time.

SERVES 2

4 celery stalks
Large chunk of fresh ginger root
¼ head of lettuce
1 lime
150g/5 oz apple or pineapple

Using a juicer, add half the celery through the tube before juicing the rest of the celery stalks with the ginger. Next juice the lettuce with the lime then finish with the apple or pineapple, whichever one you are using. Enjoy immediately.

BAKED APPLE PIE SMOOTHIE

This tastes like dessert in a glass, creamy and spicy from the combination of cinnamon, ginger, nutmeg and vanilla. You could blend all of the ingredients raw but I find roasting brings out the sweetness of the apple pie taste more and fills your kitchen with a delicious aroma while you're waiting.

SERVES 2

½ tsp ground cinnamon
¼ tsp ground ginger
¼ tsp ground nutmeg
Pinch of vanilla powder
1 medium apple, any variety
1 tbsp coconut oil, melted
1 cup (250ml) milk of choice (dairy, almond etc)
4 ice cubes

Preheat the oven to 180°C/350°F.
    Combine the cinnamon, ginger, nutmeg and vanilla powder in a bowl.
    Core the apple and lightly coat the skin in the melted coconut oil using a pastry brush or by rolling the apple in the oil.
    Roll the apple in the spice mix until evenly coated. Place the apple on an oven tray lined with baking paper and bake in the oven for 20 minutes or until the skin starts to crinkle and the flesh softens. Remove from the oven and set aside to cool.
    Add the apple, milk, ice cubes and any of the remaining spice mix to a blender, or use an immersion blender to process until smooth and creamy.

MATCHA TEA + PEAR SMOOTHIE

Matcha tea is enjoying its time in the spotlight and for good reason. One serving of matcha tea is said to be equivalent to 10 servings of regular green tea, with matcha tea containing 137 times more the antioxidants of standard brewed green tea. In addition to its nutritional benefits it tastes good too and gives a vibrant green colour to anything it's added to.

SERVES 2

2 pears, frozen
1 cup (30g) baby spinach leaves
1 tbsp matcha tea powder
2 tbsp ABC butter or tahini
2 cups (500ml) coconut water

Prep ahead for this recipe by coring the pears and dicing the flesh into even chunks. Freeze in ziplock bags ready to go when you need them.
    Place the pears, baby spinach, matcha tea powder, ABC butter and coconut water in a blender or use a handheld immersion blender on the highest setting. Blitz until the ingredients are combined. Serve chilled.

DRAGON FRUIT STRAWBERRY BLISS

Dragon fruit, or pitaya, is a neutrally flavoured, vibrant coloured fruit that is high in vitamin C, fibre and antioxidants. Pair it in smoothies with berries such as strawberry to enhance the flavour or simply enjoy the fruit scooped out of its skin with a spoon.

SERVES 2

½ dragon fruit/pitaya
1 cup (150g) strawberries, hulled
½ tsp vanilla powder
2 cups (500ml) filtered water

Remove the dragon fruit flesh and add to a blender with the strawberries, vanilla powder and water. Blitz until smooth, adding more water if needed.

You can replace the dragon fruit with 1-2 small cooked beetroots if you cannot source pitaya, the flavour will be earthier as dragon fruit has a very mild profile.

IMMUNITY SHOT

Everyone is after the elusive
formula for avoiding or curing
the common cold. While it is a
combination of managing stress,
diet, your environment, sleep
and just general luck sometimes,
there are certain ingredients
you can boost in your diet when you
begin feeling under the weather.
For me, ginger is the number
1 player when the temperature
drops and I find juicing a large
chunk of fresh ginger root with a
carrier, such as apple or cucumber,
and taken first thing in the
morning helps me through the
winter months. This is also a great
drink in the morning for those
wanting an energy boost without
drinking coffee.

SERVES 1

**Large chunk of fresh ginger (at least
the size of your thumb)**
½ an apple

Use a juicer or blender to combine
the largest chunk of fresh ginger
you can handle with the apple.
I prefer to juice this recipe and take
it like an actual shot, in one blow
so you can feel the burn of the fresh
ginger on your throat.

ICED CHAI TEA

Commercial iced tea is often full of refined sugar; make-at-home syrups and sachets should be avoided for the same reason. Buying good quality tea is the first step to make delicious iced drinks at home. Compliment the tea with simple flavours and allow enough time for brewing and chilling to let the tea really shine.

SERVES 2-4

1-2 chai tea bags
3-4 cups (750ml-1L) filtered water
Peel of 1 lemon
¼ cup (60ml) rice malt syrup or maple syrup
Ice to serve
Water, soda water or almond milk

In a small saucepan place the tea bag, water and lemon peel. Bring to the boil then reduce to a simmer. Remove the tea bags using tongs and stir through the rice malt syrup to desired sweetness.

Remove the tea from the heat and let it cool to room temperature before pouring into a jar or jug and chilling in the refrigerator for at least 30 minutes.

To serve, fill each glass with ice cubes, pour over the tea mixture to half way up the glass and top with water, soda water, almond milk or the milk of your choice.

BANANA + SPINACH DELIGHT

Hide the greens in this creamy banana smoothie that's a cinch to whip up in the morning when you're on the run or when you want to slow things down and sip and savour the flavours. Banana is a great smoothie base as it adds a creamy texture and sweet flavour, pair the banana with a nut butter of choice and you have a decadent, protein-rich drink.

SERVES 1

1 banana, frozen
1 cup (30g) baby spinach leaves
1 cup (250ml) coconut milk
½ cup (125ml) filtered water
1 tsp ground cinnamon

Add all the ingredients to a blend and pulse on high until smooth and creamy.

PAPAYA + PASSIONFRUIT KISS

This smoothie is perfect for a hot day to boost your energy and refresh you. Leaving some of the papaya seeds in the smoothie will give a peppery taste so decide whether you blend them in or not based on personal preference. I like to blend some of the seeds in then strain the smoothie before drinking so a hint of the pepper is left in.

SERVES 1

1 cup (140g) papaya, diced
2 passionfruit
1 cup (250ml) coconut milk or water
½ cup (125ml) filtered water
½ tsp vanilla powder

Add the diced papaya, the pulp and seeds from the passionfruit, the coconut milk, water and vanilla powder and blitz on high until smooth. Pour through a sieve to remove any passionfruit seeds still remaining if you don't want to drink them.

WATERMELON SMOOTHIE WITH COCONUT JELLY

Watermelon is the quintessential summer fruit, so refreshing and abundant at the market during the warmer months. Pairing the sweet fruit with coconut jelly creates a healthy bubble tea-type drink at home, without the excess sugar and unknown ingredients.

SERVES 1-2

COCONUT JELLY
1 cup (250ml) coconut water
1½ tsp grass fed gelatine

2 cups (300g) watermelon, cubed + frozen
1 tbsp coconut oil
¼ cup (60ml) fresh lime juice
Handful of fresh mint leaves

Prepare the coconut jelly ahead of time. In a small saucepan over low heat combine the coconut water and gelatine; stir until the gelatine has dissolved. Pour the liquid into a shallow tray lined with baking paper and set in the refrigerator for at least 2 hours.

Buy fresh watermelon, cube and store in ziplock bags in the freezer ready for use. In a blender combine the watermelon, coconut oil, lime juice and mint leaves. There should be enough water in the watermelon without having to add any more but if you want to adjust the consistency of the smoothie add a small amount of water or coconut water at a time.

When ready to serve, take the coconut jelly out of the fridge and dice into small cubes. Evenly divide the jellies between two glasses and top with the watermelon smoothie. Serve with wide straws to suck the jellies up.

SPICED PEACH CRUMBLE SMOOTHIE

Drinks that taste like dessert are always popular, and a late-summer peach smoothie when the fruit is ripe and readily available is always a good idea. You can substitute pumpkin for the peach during cooler months for a similar result. Enjoy the smoothie as is or with the crumble topping for added crunch.

SERVES 1

1 ripe peach, pitted
½ banana, frozen
1 cup (250ml) almond milk
1 tbsp almond butter
1 tsp ground cinnamon
¼ tsp ground ginger

CRUMBLE TOPPING
¼ cup (40g) almonds
1 tbsp rice malt syrup
½ tsp vanilla powder

Prepare the crumble topping by blitzing the almonds in the bowl of a food processor until a chunky crumb forms. Stir through the rice malt syrup and vanilla powder then spread on an oven tray lined with baking paper and bake for 10 minutes at 180°C/350°F or until crisp. Set aside to cool.

For the smoothie, dice the peach into even-sized chunks and add to a blender with the banana, almond milk, almond butter, cinnamon and ginger. Blitz until smooth and creamy. Serve in a tall glass with the crumble on top.

STRAWBERRY QUINOA CAKE SMOOTHIE

So it's not quite a strawberry shortcake but it's a sweet start to the day or can be enjoyed as an afternoon treat, and is packed full of fresh strawberries, creamy coconut milk and fibre-packed quinoa flakes, to help see you through to the next meal.

SERVES 1

150g/5 oz fresh strawberries, hulled
1 cup (250ml) coconut milk
½ tsp vanilla powder
3 tbsp quinoa flakes

Chop the strawberries into even-sized chunks and add to a blender with the coconut milk, vanilla powder and quinoa flakes. Blitz on high until smooth and frothy. Serve immediately.

BANANA ESPRESSO SMOOTHIE

This smoothie has a special secret ingredient that takes it to a whole new level – tahini! Tahini, a sesame seed paste, is rich in minerals including magnesium and iron, is a great source of calcium, helps promote healthy cell growth and has one of the highest natural sources of lecithin, which helps to reduce the levels of fat in the blood.

SERVES 1

1 banana, frozen
1 tbsp hulled tahini
1 cup (250ml) almond milk
½ tsp ground cinnamon
1 shot of espresso coffee, chilled

In a blender or using an immersion blender, combine banana, tahini, almond milk and cinnamon and blend until smooth and creamy.

Pour into a chilled glass and stir through the espresso shot.

CHOC HAZELNUT SHAKE

A chocolate milkshake is a favourite for the young and the young at heart but is a sugar cocktail we can all afford to replace with the lighter, Real Food version below. Using coconut milk in shakes adds sweetness, thickens the mixture naturally without adding ice cream and fills you up with good fats.

SERVES 1

1 cup (250ml) coconut milk or milk of choice
2 tbsp raw cacao powder
¼ cup (35g) toasted hazelnuts, skins removed
1 tsp rice malt syrup, honey or maple syrup (optional)

Place all ingredients in a blender and blitz until smooth. Add additional sweetener if required; if you are using coconut milk taste the shake before adding any sweetener, you may find it sweet enough already.

QUINOA QUEEN

Adding quinoa to this smoothie helps bulk the drink up and keep you full, plus adds a fibre hit and helps makes the smoothie creamier.

SERVES 1

2 cups (500ml) basic nut milk (page 13)
½ cup (50g) quinoa flakes
1 banana, frozen
½ cup (75g) blueberries, fresh or frozen

Blitz everything together on high in a blender until smooth and creamy. Add additional spices if desired, such as cinnamon or nutmeg.

ORANGE PARADISE

Beta-carotene, found in orange vegetables like carrots, is great for boosting your immunity. Pair this with turmeric, a great detoxifying ingredient that can help reduce bodily inflammation, fresh orange for vitamin C, and coconut oil as a good fat to help absorb the nutrients in the fruit and vegetables, and you really do have bliss in a cup.

SERVES 2

1 large carrot
2 celery stalks, including leaves
1 orange, peeled
1 thumb-sized piece of fresh turmeric
1 tbsp coconut oil, melted

Process the carrot, celery, orange and turmeric in a juicer. Be careful when adding the turmeric as it can stain. Stir through the melted coconut oil directly before serving.

GREEN WITH ENVY

Anything naturally this green must be good for you! Cabbage is often overlooked when making juices and smoothies but is such a beneficial vegetable to include in your diet to help boost immunity and digestion, it also boasts a plethora of vitamins and antioxidants. Begin with a small amount of cabbage and increase as you like, add a small amount of turmeric to the juice if you experience stomach discomfort due to the cabbage.

SERVES 2

100g/3.5 oz green cabbage,
  cut into chunks
1 large green apple
1 cucumber
2 celery stalks, leaves included
Large chunk of ginger
1 lemon, skin removed

Process the green cabbage, apple, cucumber, celery, ginger and lemon through the juicer or blitz in a blender for a smoothie, adding water as needed to thin the consistency.

RUBY RED JUICE

Juicing beetroot is an earthy culinary experience that may take some getting used to. Juice the beet leaves if possible as they contain many beneficial vitamins and minerals while the bulb adds its beautiful red hue to the drink.

SERVES 2

1 large beetroot
3 celery stalks, including leaves
1 cup (150g) fresh raspberries
2 cups (500ml) coconut water

Cut the beetroot to size to fit through the feeding tube on your juicer. Process the beetroot, celery and raspberries through the juicer then stir through the coconut water before serving over ice.

Spring Onions
$2-
Bunch

Something
ON THE
Side

CACAO HAZELNUT SPREAD

1 cup (150g) roasted hazelnuts
2 tbsp raw cacao powder
⅓ cup (80ml) maple syrup
½ cup (125ml) coconut milk
1 tbsp coconut oil

Soak the hazelnuts in filtered water overnight, drain and rinse before placing in the bowl of a food processor or blender with the cacao powder. Blitz until a fine crumb forms then add the maple syrup, coconut milk and coconut oil and blend until smooth in consistency. Store in the refrigerator for up to two weeks.

STRAWBERRY CINNAMON CHIA JAM

300g/10.5 oz fresh strawberries, hulled
1 cinnamon stick
¼ cup (60ml) filtered water
½ cup (85g) chia seeds

Roughly dice the strawberries and add to a small saucepan with the cinnamon stick and water.

Gently heat the strawberries for 5-10 minutes until they begin to release juice and soften. Remove from the heat and let cool.

Remove the cinnamon stick from the pan and use an immersion blender, or fork to puree the strawberries to your desired consistency, leaving some chunky pieces if you like.

Stir through the chia seeds; pour the jam into a glass jar with a lid and store in the refrigerator for up to 10 days.

COCONUT HONEY BUTTER

2 cups (160g) unsweetened shredded
   coconut
½ cup (125ml) raw honey
   or sweetener of choice
Zest of 1 lemon

Place the shredded coconut
in the bowl of a food processor
fitted with the S blade attachment,
or a blender. Blend on high until
the coconut begins to form a paste,
you may need to stop occasionally
to scrape down the sides of the bowl.

Add the honey and lemon zest
and continue blending until
a smooth consistency forms. If the
mixture looks too dry keep going
as it can take a while for the butter
to form depending on your food
processor or blender. You may add
¼ cup (60ml) of water or coconut
milk to thin the consistency of the
butter out if you like.

APPLE GINGER BUTTER

2 large green apples
2 inch piece of fresh ginger
½ tsp ground cinnamon
⅓ cup (80ml) maple syrup, raw honey
  or rice malt syrup
1 cup (250ml) apple cider vinegar
½ cup (125ml) water (as needed)

Core the apple and dice it into
even chunks. Dice the ginger and
add to a saucepan with the apple,
cinnamon, sweetener of choice
and apple cider vinegar. Cook over
low heat until the apple softens,
you may need to add a small
amount of water to the mixture
during the cooking process if
it looks like it needs it. Add a little
at a time, the apples should
be moist but not covered in liquid.

When the apples and ginger are
tender, remove the pan from the
heat and use a handheld immersion
blender or food processor to puree
the mixture into a smooth butter.

Enjoy on toasted rye bread,
drizzled over your morning porridge
or added to smoothies.

ORANGE ZEST ROASTED STRAWBERRIES

250g/9 oz fresh strawberries,
  hulled
Zest of 1 large orange
¼ tsp vanilla powder

Preheat the oven to 160°C/320°F.
Slice the strawberries into even
chunks or rounds and place in
a single layer on an oven tray lined
with baking paper. Sprinkle over
the orange zest and vanilla powder
and roast in the oven for 25 minutes
until the strawberries are soft and
their colour has intensified.

Store in an airtight jar or container
in the fridge and use to top porridge,
granola or desserts.

CHILLI + SUMAC PEPITA CRUMBLE

⅔ cup (120g) pepitas/pumpkin
  seeds
1 tbsp ground sumac
1 tsp dried chilli flakes
1 tbsp coconut oil, melted
Pinch of sea salt

In a bowl combine the pepitas,
sumac, chilli flakes, coconut oil
and sea salt. Heat a small pan over
a low flame then add the pepita
mixture and toast until the mixture
is fragrant and the pepitas begin
to pop, about 5 minutes. Transfer
the mixture to the bowl of a food
processor and blitz into a crumble.
Serve over salads for extra crunch.

SAFFRON YOGHURT WITH DUKKAH CRUMB

DUKKAH
½ cup (50g) shelled pistachios
  (or other nuts or seeds of choice)
2 tbsp coriander seeds
2 tbsp cumin seeds
1 tbsp sesame seeds
1 tsp sea salt
Pinch of black peppercorns

Pinch of saffron threads or 1 tsp
  ground turmeric
½ cup (125g) natural Greek
  yoghurt

Prepare the dukkah by blitzing the
pistachios, coriander, cumin, sesame
seeds, salt and pepper in a food
processor or by hand using a mortar
and pestle.

Soak the saffron threads in 1 tbsp
of warm water until the colour is
released (approximately 5 minutes).
Stir through the natural yoghurt.
Alternatively, stir the turmeric
through the yoghurt. Sprinkle
the dukkah over the top of the
yoghurt. Serve with vegetable sticks
for dipping.

CHOCOLATE BUCKINIS

1 cup (150g) buckinis
1 tbsp raw cacao powder
1 tsp vanilla powder
1 tbsp rice malt syrup

Preheat the oven to 160°C/320°F and line an oven tray with baking paper. In a bowl combine the buckinis, cacao powder, vanilla powder and rice malt syrup and stir until the buckinis are completely coated. Spread the mixture out onto the oven tray and bake for 15-20 minutes until crisp but not burnt. Set aside to cool then crumble into large chunks. Store in an airtight container for up to two weeks.

SALTED STICKY DATE ICE CREAM SAUCE

6 Medjool dates, pitted
1 tsp vanilla powder
1 cup (250ml) coconut milk
½ tsp sea salt

Blitz the dates, vanilla powder and coconut milk in a food processor or blender until smooth. Pour the mixture into a small saucepan and gently heat until warm. Add the sea salt, stir through and then pour the warm sauce over ice cream to serve.

WHIPPED VANILLA COCONUT CREAM

1 cup (200g) coconut cream solids (from the top of the can)
1½ tsp vanilla powder
2 tbsp maple syrup (optional)

Chill the coconut cream in the fridge overnight. When ready, place the chilled coconut cream, vanilla powder and maple syrup in the bowl of a stand mixer, or use hand beaters and whisk until thick, about 10 minutes. Use straight away.

VEGETABLE CHIPS

While the convenience of opening a bag of chips is undeniable, the list of less than ideal ingredients is equally hard to refute. You can easily make your own vegetable chips by finely slicing a selection of root vegetables and roasting them on high in the oven, seasoning with your own mix of spices to taste.

SERVES 2

1 large beetroot
1 large sweet potato
1 parsnip
3 tbsp coconut oil, melted
2 tsp sea salt
Spices to season: choose from cinnamon, cumin, paprika, chilli, sumac etc

Preheat the oven to 200°C/400°F and line an oven tray with baking paper.

Wash and thoroughly dry the vegetables – you can peel the skin off but I prefer to leave it on. Using a mandolin slicer, slice the vegetables on the thinnest setting. You can also use a knife for this, just try and keep the slices as thin and uniform as possible.

Lay the vegetable slices in a single layer on the tray and drizzle the coconut oil over the top. You want to lightly coat the vegetables but not drown them in oil or they will take longer to crisp up. Sprinkle over the sea salt and any additional seasonings you are using and roast the chips in the oven for 10 minutes before turning the chips over and roasting for an additional 5-10 minutes, keeping an eye on them so they don't burn. Remove the chips from the oven and set on a wire rack to cool.

The chips are best enjoyed fresh from the oven although can be stored in an airtight container or ziplock bag for another day or two, they will just lose their crunch.

CREAMED SPINACH

200g/7 oz baby spinach leaves
2 tbsp chives, roughly chopped
2 garlic cloves, minced
1 spring onion/scallion, roughly sliced
½ cup (125ml) coconut milk

Wilt the baby spinach in a pan then add the chives, minced garlic and spring onion and cook until fragrant and tender, about 4 minutes. Add the coconut milk to the pan and heat gently for a further 2 minutes.

Serve warm as is or use an immersion blender or food processor to puree the spinach mixture until smooth.

CHEAT'S PICKLED GINGER

Medium chunk of fresh ginger root
1 tbsp raw honey
1 tbsp rice wine vinegar
2 tbsp apple cider vinegar

Peel the ginger and finely slice it using a mandolin slicer or a knife, the thinner you can get the ginger the better.

Place the ginger in a small saucepan with the honey, rice wine vinegar and apple cider vinegar over a low heat. Stir until the honey has dissolved then simmer until the mixture has reduced by half, at least 25 minutes.

Place the ginger and liquid in a small dish in the fridge to cool down for at least 30 minutes before eating, although it is softer if left to sit overnight.

BAKED HALOUMI WITH CHILLI + MINT

250g/7 oz haloumi cheese
1 long red chilli
Handful of fresh mint leaves
Juice from 1 lemon

Preheat the oven to 180°C/350°F and place the haloumi on an oven tray lined with baking paper.

In a food processor blitz the chilli, fresh mint and lemon juice together to create a marinade. Pour over the haloumi and bake in the oven for 15-20 minutes until the haloumi is golden brown and soft.

Serve as a snack, as part of an appetiser board or sliced and added to a salad.

CHILLI PUMPKIN + GOAT CHEESE SPREAD

You can substitute the pumpkin in this recipe with carrot or sweet potato for a similar taste and texture. You can also omit the butter and replace with 1 tbsp of hulled tahini to help add a depth of flavour to the steamed vegetable. When you compare the simple list of ingredients below to the ingredients list on the back of a tub of dip at the supermarket, you will discover how easy, satisfying and healthy making your own dips and spreads at home is, and all for a fraction of the cost of store-bought.

200g/7 oz pumpkin (any variety)
1½ tbsp dried chilli flakes
½ tbsp unsalted butter
2 tbsp goat cheese

Remove the skin from the pumpkin and dice the flesh into even sized chunks. Steam the pumpkin for 5-6 minutes, either in a microwave or in a steamer basket on the stove top over simmering water.

Once the pumpkin is tender add the chilli flakes and butter. Use an immersion blender to blitz the mixture to a smooth consistency.

Add the goat cheese to a small bowl and stir vigorously until the cheese is a smooth paste.

Pour the pumpkin spread into a serving dish and gently stir through the goat cheese to create a marbled effect. Serve as a spread on fresh rye bread or as a dip for vegetable sticks.

ZUCCHINI HUMMUS

2 medium zucchinis/courgettes
Extra virgin olive oil
Pinch of sea salt and black pepper
2-3 heaped tbsp hulled tahini
¼ cup (10g) fresh dill
¼ cup (60ml) fresh lemon juice

Preheat the oven to 180°C/350°F.

Slice the zucchini in half lengthways, place on an oven tray lined with baking paper, drizzle a small amount of olive oil over the top and season with a pinch of sea salt and black pepper. Roast in the oven for 30 minutes until soft.

Place the zucchini, tahini, dill and lemon juice in the bowl of a food processor or use a stick mixer to blend into a smooth consistency. Store in the refrigerator for up to one week.

LEMON HUMMUS

200g/7 oz cooked chickpeas
1 tbsp hulled tahini
Juice + zest of ½ a lemon
¼-½ cup (60-125ml) extra virgin olive oil or water
Sea salt and black pepper

Add the chickpeas, tahini, lemon juice and zest to the bowl of a food processor with the feed tube open. Pour in a little olive oil at a time as you mix on medium speed. The amount of oil added will depend on the consistency you want the hummus. Blend until smooth, taste then season with sea salt and black pepper. You could also add a garlic clove to the mixture or spices such as smoked paprika or cumin.

AVOCADO WHITE BEAN SMASH

1 medium avocado
½ cup (100g) cooked cannellini beans (or other white bean)
¼ cup (60ml) fresh lemon juice
¼ cup (10g) flat leaf parsley, finely chopped
1 tsp chilli flakes (or fresh chilli)
1 tsp sea salt

In a mixing bowl combine the avocado flesh, cannellini beans, lemon juice, parsley, chilli and salt. Use the back of a fork to roughly mash the ingredients together. You can use an immersion blender to do this but I like to keep some texture to the dish and a fork does this easily. Serve on toasted rye bread or as a dip for fresh vegetables.

BABA GANOUSH DIP

2 large eggplants/aubergines
Extra virgin olive oil
3 tsp sea salt
1 tbp smoked paprika
1 tsp ground cumin
2 garlic cloves
2 tbsp hulled tahini

Preheat the oven to 180°C/350°F.

Prick each eggplant several times with a fork, knife or skewer. Using a gas burner, BBQ hotplate or a grill/broiler, char the skin of the eggplants for 5 minutes to help create a smoky flavour.

Transfer the eggplants to a baking dish or oven tray, drizzle the olive oil over the top and sprinkle over the sea salt, smoked paprika and cumin. Add the garlic cloves to the tray and roast for 30 minutes or until soft and caramelised.

Add the eggplants, including the skin, and the garlic to the bowl of a food processor and blitz with the tahini until smooth. for 30 minutes or until soft and caramelised.

Add the eggplants, including the skin, and the garlic to the bowl of a food processor and blitz with the tahini until smooth.

Fabulous fermentation

Fermenting fresh vegetables, such as the humble cabbage, is a great way to provide beneficial probiotics to your gut as well as delivering a tasty addition to your plate. Basic fermenting at home is easy, and once you're confident with sauerkraut and kim chi you can begin experimenting with more complicated recipes. When starting out, aim to make smaller batches as you hone your skills and discover what tastes you like.

RED CABBAGE + BEETROOT KRAUT

½ head red cabbage
2 golden or red beetroot
2 tsp sea salt

Remove the core from the cabbage, reserve a couple of outer leaves to the side, and finely slice the remaining cabbage leaves. Trim the beetroot ends, wash the skins and finely slice into batons or rounds.

Add the cabbage and beetroot to a large bowl and massage the salt through the mixture. It is a good idea to wear rubber or disposable gloves during this stage as the beetroot and red cabbage can stain your skin temporarily. Keep massaging until the cabbage is tender.

Sterilise a large glass jar with boiling water then stuff the cabbage and beetroot in, pushing down to fit as much into the jar as possible. Roll up the reserved cabbage leaves and place on top of the kraut to keep the cabbage submerged in its own liquid.

As with regular sauerkraut, either place a piece of muslin cloth over the open jar, loosely place the lid on top or secure the lid and the open jar each day to release the building pressure. Store on the kitchen counter for 3 days then move to the fridge.

SIMPLE KIM CHI

1 large wombok/Chinese cabbage or white cabbage
¼ cup (20g) sea salt
Filtered water
4 garlic cloves
1 inch piece of ginger
4 long red chillis
2 tbsp water
1 large daikon/radish
2 large carrots
3 spring onions/scallions

Remove the core from the cabbage and slice the remaining leaves, either finely or into medium sized chunks. Add the cabbage and salt to a large bowl and massage with your hands to soften the leaves. Pour enough water into the bowl to just cover the cabbage and weigh it down with a plate. At this stage you can leave the cabbage to rest anywhere from 1 hour to overnight.

Rinse the cabbage in fresh filtered water to remove the excess salt then thoroughly drain the cabbage. Wash the soaking bowl then add the cabbage back in.

Add the garlic, ginger, chilli and water to the bowl of a food processor and blitz into a paste, adding more water if necessary.

Finely chop or shred the daikon, carrots and spring onion and add to the bowl of cabbage. At this stage you may want to wear rubber or disposable gloves as you add the chilli mixture to the cabbage and work it through the vegetables.

Sterilise a large glass jar with boiling water then stuff the kim chi mix into it, pushing down hard to compact it. There should be a small amount of liquid covering the top of the kim chi at this point. Seal the jar and leave it to ferment on the kitchen counter for 3-5 days before storing it in the fridge for a further week before eating. The flavour will intensify the longer it is left so taste it after a week to see if it's to your liking or if it needs more time.

BASIC SAUERKRAUT

¼-½ head of savoy cabbage
2 tbsp sea salt flakes
1 tsp caraway seeds

Remove the core from the cabbage, reserve 1 or 2 outer leaves to the side and finely slice the rest of the leaves. Add the cabbage to a large bowl with the salt and caraway seeds and massage with your hands for 5 minutes. As you work the salt into the leaves you will notice liquid forming at the bottom of the bowl, keep massaging until the cabbage has soften and is damp.

Sterilise a medium sized glass jar in boiling water then stuff the cabbage firmly into the jar, pushing down to compact it as much as possible, leaving a good couple of inches at the top of the jar. Fold the reserved cabbage leaves in half and stuff into the top of the jar to weigh the sauerkraut down.

At this stage you can place a piece of muslin cloth over the top of the jar, loosely place the jar lid on top, or secure the jar lid. Store the sauerkraut on your kitchen bench for three days before moving it to the fridge. If you have secured a lid on the jar, open the jar every day while it's on the bench to release the gas forming.

Once in the fridge the sauerkraut can be enjoyed on top of scrambled eggs for breakfast, in salads, or simply a forkful at a time. Be careful not to double dip, rather remove a portion from the jar then eat, instead of returning the fork into the kraut again and again, this will help avoid contamination and early spoilage.

Eat kim chi
with a bowl
of fresh greens
or try sauerkraut
with dill +
pickled cucumber

Fill
ME
Up

CAULIFLOWER + HORSERADISH SOUP

This creamy soup has a delicious bite thanks to the addition of horseradish. It can be hard to source fresh horseradish so if you can't find any, substitute with a good quality horseradish cream, taking time to read the ingredients list and choosing the brand with no added sugar and preferably no seed oils. You could also substitute the horseradish for fresh chilli or wasabi, which will give you a different sort of heat but will still compliment the soup nicely.

SERVES 4

1 head of cauliflower
2 parsnips or potatoes, cleaned but
   not peeled
25g/1 oz butter
8 cups (2L) vegetable stock plus
   additional water as needed
3 tbsp fresh horseradish, grated
1 bunch of fresh chives
Sea salt and black pepper

Remove the florets from the cauliflower and dice the stalk into small chunks. Clean the parsnip, discard the ends and dice into even chunks. Add the cauliflower, parsnip and butter to a large stockpot and sweat for 10 minutes with a pinch of sea salt before adding the vegetable stock and cooking over a medium heat for 1 hour, until the vegetables are tender.

Add the horseradish and chives to the soup then puree the mixture using an immersion blender, making sure there are no chunks of vegetables left. If the soup is too thick, add a dash of water at a time until you reach the desired consistency. Taste the soup and season with salt and pepper if needed.

BEEF BONE BROTH

Bone broth is a great addition to your daily diet for a number of reasons. Firstly, it's extremely economical to make; it's also incredibly easy, it's just a matter of adding everything to the pot and leaving it to simmer and bubble away for hours on end. Bone broth is packed full of minerals that we often miss out on in diets that are more centred on fillets of meat and not the whole animal. Studies suggest that including bone broth in your diet helps you better absorb other proteins, and the gelatine extracted from the bones is great for your joints, skin and hair. By freezing the broth in ice cube trays, you can pop a couple of cubes out at a time and heat them up for a warming drink when you don't want to use the broth for a soup or stew.

1.5kg/3 lb grass fed beef bones
¼ cup (60ml) apple cider vinegar
Enough filtered water to cover the
   bones
1 large brown onion
2 carrots
4 celery stalks, including leaves
1 star anise
6 peppercorns
Stalks from 1 bunch of parsley

Preheat the oven to 180°C/350°F.
   Place the beef bones in a large ovenproof stockpot or dish with the apple cider vinegar. Let it sit for half an hour. Add the brown onion, carrots and celery to the pot and roast in the oven for one hour.
   Place the pot over a medium heat and add enough filtered water to cover the bones and vegetables, then add the star anise and peppercorns. Bring the mixture to the boil then reduce the heat to low.

Cook the broth on low for at least 8 hours, topping up the liquid in the pot with additional water as needed so the bones are consistently covered. If you have a slow cooker you can cook the broth on low overnight, which will help draw out even more minerals and collagen. It's easy to set the slow cooker for 8 hours during the day then follow it up with 8 hours overnight, which will give you premium bone broth with minimal effort.
   When ready, strain the bones, vegetables, star anise and peppercorns from the liquid. Store some broth in a jar in the refrigerator to be consumed within 24 hours. If you're not immediately using the rest for a soup or stew then pour any remaining broth into freezer-friendly containers or ice cube trays for later use.

CREAMY CHICKEN SOUP

Chicken noodle soup is a classic dish, great to warm you up on a cold day or pick you up when you're feeling under the weather. Making your own chicken stock is easy and allows you to control the level of salt in it as well as guaranteeing that your chicken is free range and, if possible, pasture raised, which all adds to a better taste and a more nutrient dense stock. Replace traditional wheat noodles or pasta with spiralised zucchini for an additional serve of vegetables.

SERVES 6

STOCK
1 free-range chicken
2 brown onions
2 carrots
2 celery stalks, with leaves
2 inch piece of fresh ginger
16 cups (4L) filtered water, plus more as needed

25g/1 oz grass fed butter
2 celery stalks, finely diced
2 large carrots, finely diced
Sea salt and black pepper
1 cup (250ml) coconut milk
1 zucchini/courgette, julienned or spiralised

Make the stock by adding the chicken, onions, carrots, celery, ginger and water to a large stock pot and simmering over a low to medium heat for 3-4 hours. The water should cover the chicken, if not add more as needed to submerge it. Strain the chicken and vegetables from the broth, set the chicken aside to cool and the broth aside to use later. Once cooled, shred the chicken meat from the carcass.

In a stock pot or saucepan, melt the butter then add the celery and carrots, cook for 5 minutes. Pour in the premade stock followed by the shredded chicken. Cook for 20 minutes until the vegetables are tender. Season with sea salt and ground black pepper, remembering your stock is neutral at this point so you may need to season, taste and adjust to your palate.

Just before serving stir through the coconut milk and zucchini, which will act as your noodles.

ROASTED TOMATO + THYME SOUP

Tomato soup from a can is a great comfort food but can be a source of excess salt and even sugar. This is a simple but flavourful soup that comes easily together on a busy weeknight or lazy weekend. Make a big batch of the soup, divide into smaller containers and freeze for later – no more reaching for a can of soup when pressed for time!

SERVES 4

1kg/2 lb tomatoes, any variety
8 sprigs of thyme
1 onion, diced
3 garlic cloves
3 tbsp extra virgin olive oil
2 tsp smoked paprika
2 tsp sea salt
1 tsp black pepper
4 cups (1L) beef stock (page 77)

Preheat the oven to 180°C/350°F.

Evenly slice the tomatoes into chunks and place in a deep ovenproof dish with the thyme, onion and garlic. Drizzle with olive oil, smoked paprika, sea salt and black pepper.

Over a medium flame, begin by cooking the tomatoes on the stovetop for 10-15 minutes before transferring to the oven and roasting for a further 30-40 minutes. Remove the dish from the oven and add the beef stock. Using an immersion blender, puree the soup until smooth.

For a spin on this recipe, add a long red chilli to the roasting pan and puree, seeds and all, for a spicy tomato soup. Serve with a swirl of coconut milk to dissipate the heat if needed.

SPICY BEEF + TUSCAN KALE STEW

This warming stew is simply a matter of throwing everything in the pot and giving it time. Keeping the ingredients list short allows each flavour to truly shine. Adjust the spiciness of the dish to suit your taste or omit the chillis entirely for a milder dish. You can add extra vegetables beyond the kale and pumpkin, stir through a tin of chickpeas or serve on a bed of mashed potato.

SERVES 2-4

500g/1 lb sirloin or rump steak
½ Spanish/red onion, finely
    chopped
1 inch piece of fresh ginger root,
    finely grated
4 garlic cloves, crushed
2-3 red chillis (any variety), finely
    chopped
1 cup (250g) diced tomatoes
2 cups (500ml) beef stock (page 77),
    plus more stock or water
    as needed
300g/10.5 oz pumpkin, any variety
1 bunch of Tuscan kale

Slice the beef into thin strips or cut into chunks and sprinkle lightly with sea salt. Heat up a large cast iron pot or saucepan over a medium heat. Add a drizzle of extra virgin olive oil and add the onion, ginger, garlic and chilli. Sweat for 3-5 minutes. Add the beef, tomatoes and stock, stir and reduce the heat to low. Cut the pumpkin into chunks and add to the pot. Simmer for 35 minutes until the beef is tender, checking every 15 minutes and adding additional stock or water as needed.

Remove the stem from the Tuscan kale and cut the leaves into medium sized chunks. Add the kale to the stew and cook for 20 minutes before serving.

POTATO + SNOW PEA GREEN CURRY

Making a curry paste at home is incredibly simple with the help of a food processor to blitz everything together for you but you can also use a mortar and pestle along with a little elbow grease. Make the paste ahead of time, such as on the weekend, store in an airtight jar or container in the fridge and you'll have it ready to go for a mid-week meal. You can mix up the ingredients by replacing the potato with pumpkin, sweet potato or cauliflower, or add chicken and beef if you're not going meat free.

SERVES 4

CURRY PASTE

1 lemongrass stalk
1 inch chunk of galangal
1 inch chunk of fresh ginger
Handful of fresh Thai basil leaves
2-4 green chillis (depending on desired heat)
4 garlic cloves
2 shallots
2 coriander/cilantro roots, washed
1 tbsp ground coriander
1 tbsp ground cumin
⅓ cup (80ml) olive oil, plus more as needed
Pinch of sea salt

8 medium potatoes
2 cups (500ml) coconut milk
300g/10.5 oz snow peas, trimmed
1 cup (250ml) filtered water, plus more as needed

Prepare the curry paste by removing the outer leaves of the lemongrass and cutting the stalk into chunks. Add the lemongrass to the bowl of a food processor or blender along with the galangal, ginger, basil leaves, chillis, garlic, shallots, coriander root, ground coriander, cumin, olive oil and sea salt. Blitz until a paste forms, stopping every now and then to scrape down the sides of the bowl and add a touch more oil for lubrication if needed.

Heat a large pot on medium on the stove then add the curry paste and cook until it becomes fragrant, 3-5 minutes. Pour in the coconut milk and stir to remove any stuck on bits on the bottom of the pan.

Dice the potato, skin on, into even chunks and add to the pan of sauce. Stir to coat the potatoes then reduce the heat to low, cover the pot with a lid and let the curry simmer for 45 minutes, checking occasionally and adding a dash of water if the mixture is drying up.

Top and tail the snow peas and add to the curry once the potatoes are tender. Stir through, taste and season with additional sea salt or black pepper if needed. Cook for a further 15 minutes before removing from the heat so as not to overcook the snow peas.

Serve the curry with rice, quinoa or on its own, with finely sliced snow peas on top for an optional garnish.

SIMPLE EGGPLANT + SPINACH CURRY

This curry doesn't compromise on taste but it simple and speedy, making it ideal for a busy weeknight meal. It is a great recipe to have under your belt for when supplies are running low, you can simply use leftover vegetables you have on hand.

SERVES 4

1 brown onion, diced
Extra virgin olive oil
350g/12 oz baby spinach leaves
1 medium eggplant/aubergine, diced
1 inch piece of ginger, grated
1 tsp ground cumin
1 tsp ground turmeric
1 tsp ground coriander
1 cup (250ml) coconut milk
400g/14 oz cooked chickpeas (optional)

In a medium saucepan, soften the onion in olive oil before adding the spinach and wilting.

Add the eggplant, ginger, cumin, turmeric and coriander and cook for 15-20 minutes until soft and fragrant.

Add the coconut milk and chickpeas, if using, stir and cook for a further 5 minutes. Test that the eggplant is tender then serve on its own or over rice, mashed vegetables or quinoa.

GINGER CARROT SOUP

This soup can be made with regular vegetable stock or the stock recipe below, which I developed when cooking this soup for my sister who had just been put on a low FODMAP diet, that meant no onion or celery to flavour the soup, and explains why you just use the green tops of the spring onions. The final product is a zingy and warming soup that could be topped with crunchy seeds or a drizzle of basil pesto if you felt like getting fancy.

SERVES 6

STOCK
½ lemongrass stalk
4 fresh coriander/cilantro roots, washed
2 large carrots
2 bay leaves
4 spring onions/scallions, just the green tops
2 inch chunk of fresh ginger
8 cups (2L) filtered water, plus more as needed
2 tbsp sea salt

4 carrots, washed not peeled
4 parsnips, washed not peeled
2 inch chunk of fresh ginger, grated
1 cup (50g) fresh coriander/cilantro leaves
1 cup (250ml) coconut milk
Sea salt and black pepper

Prepare the stock by adding the lemongrass, coriander roots, carrots, bay leaves, spring onions, ginger and water to a large stockpot and heating over medium for 1 hour. Add the sea salt and heat for a further 15 minutes before straining the liquid and setting aside.

Dice the carrot and parsnips into even chunks and add to a large stockpot with 1 tbsp of olive oil. Over a medium heat, sweat the vegetables for 4 minutes until softened then stir through the grated ginger and cook for a further minute.

Add the stock and coriander leaves and cook for 25 minutes, making sure the carrot and parsnip are soft and cooked through. Using an immersion blender, or blending the soup in batches, blitz the mixture until smooth. Stir through the coconut milk, taste and adjust seasoning with sea salt and black pepper if needed.

ROASTED GARLIC AND BROCCOLI CREAM SOUP

This soup is obviously not a recipe for people concerned about garlic breath and so is not an ideal choice to cook a new romantic interest. For those of us unapologetic about such things this soup is perfect any time of the year, either piping hot and nourishing in the cooler months or served lukewarm or chilled in summer.

SERVES 4

2 heads of garlic
Extra virgin olive oil
1 head of broccoli
2 celery stalks
1 leek
6 cups (1.5L) vegetable stock
1 cup (40g) flat leaf parsley leaves
1 cup (250ml) coconut milk
Sea salt and black pepper

Prepare the roasted garlic by preheating the oven to 180°C/350°F and lining an oven tray with baking paper. Cut the top off each garlic bulb to reveal the tips of the cloves. Place the heads on the oven tray and drizzle extra virgin olive oil over the top. Roast for 25 minutes or until the garlic is browned and soft but not burnt. Remove from the oven and set aside to cool.

Remove the florets from the broccoli and dice the stalk into small pieces. Dice the celery and leek and add to a large stockpot with the broccoli and a pinch of sea salt. Drizzle 1-2 tbsp of extra virgin olive oil in and sweat the vegetables until soft, about 10 minutes. Pour in the vegetable stock, stir and simmer for 1 hour.

Once the heads of garlic have cooled, squeeze out the roasted bulbs into a bowl. Take half of the roasted garlic and add to the stockpot with the parsley, reserve the remaining garlic to garnish the soup with.

Use an immersion blender, puree the soup until smooth then stir through the coconut milk and return to a low heat until ready to serve. Top each bowl of soup with some of the roasted garlic cloves.

Souper toppings

You can elevate a soup from simple to sensational with some basic toppings that are easy to whip up and sure to impress. Make the toppings ahead of time and store in airtight containers in the fridge or cupboard for when your meal needs a little inspiration.

GARLIC CASHEW CREAM

Roast 1 head of garlic in the oven at 180°C/350°F for 25 minutes until soft and caramelised. Set aside to cool then squeeze the garlic cloves out from their skins.

Soak 1 cup (150g) of cashews in boiling water for 20 minutes, drain and rinse under fresh water.

Add the cashews to the bowl of a food processor or blender with 1 cup (250ml) of filtered water, the roasted garlic, and 1 tsp each of ground black pepper and sea salt. Blitz until smooth and creamy, store in an airtight container in the fridge for up to one week.

CRISPY ONIONS

Peel the skin of one large onion, discard and cut the onion into quarters. Peel each of the onion layers away so you're left with little chip-sized pieces.

In a pan over high heat, melt ½ cup (125ml) of coconut oil. Add the onion in batches and cook for 2-3 minutes, turning with a pair of tongs until crispy.

Remove from the pan and place on a plate lined with paper towel to absorb excess oil. Sprinkle over a mixture of 1 tsp sea salt and 1 tsp smoky paprika and toss to coat.

FETA + DILL CRUMBLE

Crumble 100g/3.5 oz of Greek feta into a bowl. Finely slice ⅓ cup (25g) of fresh dill and add to the bowl with a pinch of sea salt and ½ tsp ground coriander, stir gently to combine. Store leftovers in an airtight container in the fridge for a couple of days.

SUNFLOWER SEED CUMIN CRUNCH

Take 1 cup (140g) of sunflower seeds/kernels and add to the bowl of a food processor with 2 tsp ground cumin and a pinch of sea salt. Blitz into a chunky crumb and toast in a dry pan for 3-4 minutes until fragrant.

MAPLE PEPITAS

Preheat the oven to 180°C/350°F and line an oven tray with baking paper. Combine 1 cup (120g) of pepitas/pumpkin seeds with 1½ tbsp of maple syrup and ½ tsp of sea salt. Spread the mixture evenly over the oven tray and bake for 10 minutes.

BASIL PESTO

In the bowl of a food processor blitz 1 bunch of fresh basil with 1 garlic clove, ¼ cup (60ml) of lemon juice, a good pinch of sea salt and ground black pepper, and enough extra virgin olive oil to help the mixture emulsify. I tend to skip the cheese and nuts commonly found in pestos but you could add 1 tbsp of a nut butter of your choice for an added depth of flavour. The amount of oil you use is up to you, start with ⅓ cup (80ml) and add as you go, you may prefer a chunkier pesto or you may want to take it all the way to pouring stage to drizzle over your soup. Store any leftovers in an airtight container in the fridge for up to one week.

PUMPKIN + PROSCIUTTO SALAD

This is a great flavour combination, with sweet and spicy pumpkin mixed with the salty prosciutto. This salad is a great accompaniment to roasted chicken, or you can omit the prosciutto and serve with falafels for a vegetarian option.

SERVES 2

250g/9 oz pumpkin, any variety
2 tbsp coconut oil
1 tbsp dried chilli flakes
2 tsp smoked paprika
2 cups (130g) baby kale leaves
150g/5 oz thinly sliced prosciutto
   or pancetta
Pepitas/pumpkin seeds to serve

Preheat the oven to 180°C/350°F and line an oven tray with baking paper.
   Slice the pumpkin into chunks or crescents of an even thickness and spread out on the tray. Pour over the coconut oil, chilli flakes and paprika. Roast in the oven for 30-40 minutes or until soft and slightly caramelised on top.
   On a platter, spread out the baby kale and half the prosciutto slices. Place the roasted pumpkin on top then scatter the remaining prosciutto around. Top the salad with pepitas for extra crunch.

SIMPLE TUNA SALAD

When you hear tuna salad you might picture a can of tuna emptied onto a plate with a few leaves and seasonings. It's not hard to cook a tuna steak at home if you have access to good quality fresh tuna. Keep the salad simple with additional seasonings so you can really appreciate the natural flavour of the fish.

SERVES 1

8 cherry tomatoes
1 small cucumber
¼ Spanish/red onion
150g-180g/5-6 oz fresh tuna steak
Sea salt and black pepper
Extra virgin olive oil

In a pan, drizzle a small amount of extra virgin olive oil and cook the cherry tomatoes for 3-4 minutes until the skin begins to darken and the tomatoes soften. Set aside.
   Dice the cucumber and finely slice the Spanish onion.
   Season both sides of the tuna steak with sea salt and black pepper; use your hands to press the seasoning into the flesh.
   Heat a small pan with a drizzle of extra virgin olive oil. Lay the tuna steak into the hot pan away from you and cook for 1-2 minutes each side. Set aside to rest on a plate for 4 minutes.
   Slice the tuna steak and assemble the salad by laying the tuna on top of the tomatoes, cucumber and Spanish onion. Drizzle a small amount of extra virgin olive oil or fresh lemon juice over the top if desired.

AVOCADO, HALOUMI + RASPBERRY SALAD

This is such a great combination of flavours; it can be served alongside a protein of choice, such as chicken, or enjoyed on its own. The nutty avocado mixed with the sweet raspberries and salty haloumi ensures every mouthful of this salad is a delight.

SERVES 2

250g/9 oz haloumi, diced
1 ripe avocado, diced
250g/9 oz fresh raspberries
Extra virgin olive oil
1 tbsp fresh lemon juice
Sea salt and black pepper

In a small pan, cook the haloumi until brown. You may add a small drizzle of olive oil to help crisp the cheese up but it is not necessary.
   Make the salad by combining diced avocado and fresh raspberries with the cooked haloumi. To bulk up the salad add bitter greens such as rocket (arugula).
   Drizzle a small amount of extra virgin olive oil and fresh lemon juice over the top and season with a pinch of sea salt and a good grinding of fresh black pepper. Gently toss before serving.

ROASTED SWEET POTATOES WITH CAULIFLOWER TABOULI

Roasted potatoes in their jackets is a great meal whether it's warm or cold outside. You can replace sweet potatoes with white potatoes in this recipe, or fill roasted capsicums/peppers with the cauliflower tabouli. In cooler months you can still fill the potatoes with tabouli or try making a simple ratatouille with diced vegetables in a tomato sauce, roasting alongside the sweet potato and then filling the potato with the mixture.

SERVES 4

CAULIFLOWER TABOULI
½ head of cauliflower
1 large bunch of parsley
1 cup (40g) coriander/cilantro
2 spring onions/scallions
Zest of 1 lemon
1 tbsp extra virgin olive oil
Pinch of sea salt and black pepper

4 sweet potatoes
Extra virgin olive oil
Sea salt and black pepper

Preheat the oven to 180°C/350°F and line an oven tray with baking paper. Take each sweet potato and cut a long slit into it down the middle lengthways. Place the potatoes on the tray and drizzle olive oil over the top. Season with a good pinch of sea salt and grinding of black pepper. Roast in the oven for 45-60 minutes or until tender, careful not to let them burn. Remove from the oven and pry open the slit in each potato to make room for the tabouli.

Prepare the tabouli by removing the cauliflower leaves and chopping the stalks and florets into chunks. Using a food processor, pulse the cauliflower with the parsley and coriander until a fine crumb is formed. Slice the spring onion finely and stir through the tabouli. Add seasoning to the mix by adding extra virgin olive oil, lemon zest, sea salt and black pepper.

Fill each sweet potato with tabouli and serve. As an optional garnish, add pomegranate seeds and diced fresh tomato on top.

BAKED FALAFEL + CUCUMBER SALAD WITH PEPITA CRUMBLE

Falafel is such an easy dish to make that you'll no longer need to buy them premade or in a packet mix. The falafel are baked and not fried in oil, making for a lighter meal bursting with flavour from the combination of spices.

SERVES 2

FALAFEL
1 brown onion, quartered
2 cups (400g) cooked chickpeas
2 tsp ground cumin
2 tsp ground coriander
½ cup (25g) fresh coriander/cilantro
2 tbsp extra virgin olive oil
2 tbsp almond meal
1 tsp sea salt

CUCUMBER SALAD
1 large cucumber, any variety
1 tbsp sumac
Watercress, lettuce or baby spinach

PEPITA CRUMBLE
⅔ cup (120g) pepitas (pumpkin seeds)
1 tbsp coconut oil, melted
1 tsp dried chilli flakes
Pinch of sea salt

Preheat the oven to 180°C/350°F.

In the bowl of a food processor, combine the onion, chickpeas, cumin, coriander, almond meal and extra virgin olive oil. Blitz until a chunky paste forms.

Line an oven tray with baking paper and roll spoon-fuls of the falafel mix into balls in your hands. Evenly space the balls on the tray and bake in the oven for 15-20 minutes.

Dice the cucumber and toss in sumac. Rinse the watercress and add to a bowl or platter then sprinkle the cucumber and falafels evenly over the top.

Coat the pepitas in coconut oil, chilli flakes and sea salt. Heat a pan over medium and toast the pepitas until fragrant. Transfer the pepitas to the bowl of a food processor or use a mortar and pestle and blitz into a crumble. Sprinkle the pepita crumble over the top of the salad and serve.

GREEN OLIVE + FIG SALAD

When figs are in season this refreshing salad features them twice, with the plump fruit served alongside salty olives to counterbalance the sweetness, and pureed into a zingy dressing to drizzle over the top.

SERVES 2

450g/1 lb lettuce, any variety
150g/5 oz green olives of choice
4 fresh figs

DRESSING
1 fresh fig
1 tbsp lime juice
1 tbsp apple cider vinegar
½ tsp sea salt
½ tsp ground black pepper

Prepare the salad by washing the lettuce and shredding into large chunks. Place into a bowl and add the green olives and quartered figs.
 Make the dressing by scooping out the fig flesh and adding to a small bowl with the lime juice, apple cider vinegar, sea salt and black pepper. Whisk together, the mixture won't look like a lot but is enough to dot over the salad for a flavour boost.

ROASTED BRUSSELS SPROUTS WITH CHILLI TAHINI DRESSING

Even the fussiest eater will be surprised by the flavour that roasting brings out in these Brussels sprouts, and the tahini dressing is so versatile it's great drizzled over any salad or vegetable.

SERVES 2

250g/9 oz Brussels sprouts
Extra virgin olive oil
Salt and pepper to taste

TAHINI DRESSING
2 tbsp hulled tahini
2 tbsp water (plus more as needed)
2 tsp chilli flakes

Zest and juice of ½ a lemon
1 tsp paprika
1 garlic clove, crushed

Preheat the oven to 180°C/350°F and line an oven tray with baking paper.
 Trim the ends from the Brussels sprouts before coating in olive oil and a good pinch of sea salt and pepper. Roast for approximately 20 minutes until browned but not burned.
 Prepare the dressing by whisking tahini, water, lemon zest, paprika and crushed garlic in a small bowl. Serve the Brussels sprouts warm with the dressing over the top.

QUINOA "FRIED RICE"

Swap the old-school fried rice with soy sauce and shrimp for a lighter, healthier version using quinoa. This is a great recipe to make using leftover quinoa, or simply cook some for this dish. Add whatever vegetables you have on hand in the fridge or stick to the classic scrambled egg, peas, capsicum and spring onion. Serve alongside a piece of grilled meat or enjoy as a salad on its own.

SERVES 4

3 free range eggs
1 red capsicum/pepper
1 cup (120g) cooked peas
3 spring onions/scallions
2 celery stalks
Handful of coriander/cilantro leaves
2 cups (370g) cooked quinoa
Juice of 1 lemon
Sea salt and black pepper

Crack the eggs into a bowl and whisk with a fork. Heat up a small frying pan and scramble the egg until cooked to your liking. Set aside.

Dice the red capsicum, finely slice the spring onions and celery stalks and add to a bowl. Finely chop the coriander leaves and add to the bowl.

Add the cooked quinoa to the bowl followed by the lemon juice and a pinch of sea salt and black pepper. Stir through the scrambled egg until all the ingredients are combined. Leftovers will keep in an airtight container in the fridge for a couple of days.

TURMERIC ROASTED CAULIFLOWER CUPS WITH SATAY SAUCE

Serve this as a salad in bowls instead of in the lettuce cups if you prefer. You can replace the cauliflower with broccoli or Brussels sprouts. Roasting with turmeric brings out a terrific flavour and deep colour, and it's one of the best spices you can use, packed full of antioxidants and a great anti-inflammatory to help regulate insulin and balance blood glucose, plus it tastes great.

SERVES 4

½ head of cauliflower
½ cup (125ml) coconut milk
2 tsp ground turmeric
1 tsp sea salt
½ tsp ground black pepper
4 large lettuce leaves or 8 smaller leaves

SATAY SAUCE

1 cup (125g) cashews, soaked in water overnight
¼ cup (60ml) fresh lemon juice
1 tbsp Tamari/wheat free soy sauce
½ cup (125ml) hulled tahini
2 garlic cloves
Sea salt and black pepper

Preheat the oven to 180°C/350°F and line an oven tray with baking paper.

Remove the cauliflower florets from the stalk and chop into small pieces. In a small bowl combine the coconut milk, turmeric, sea salt and black pepper. Spread the cauliflower in an even layer on the tray and pour the marinade over the top. Bake in the oven for 20 minutes or until tender.

While the cauliflower is cooking, remove the leaves from the lettuce, wash, pat dry with paper towel and set aside.

Prepare the satay sauce by rinsing the soaked nuts in fresh water, straining in a sieve then adding to the bowl of a food processor along with the lemon juice, Tamari, tahini, garlic, and a pinch of salt and pepper. Blitz until a smooth paste forms, adding a touch of water as needed to thin the consistency.

Serve the roasted cauliflower in the lettuce cups with a spoonful of the satay sauce.

PRAWN + SPROUTS RICE PAPER ROLLS

Make these ahead of time for an easy grab-and-go lunch. Sub the prawns for cooked strips of chicken or beef, or keep it vegetarian and stuff the rolls full of finely sliced or shredded vegetables and leaves.

MAKES 6

12 cooked prawns, any variety
1 large carrot
½ daikon (white radish)
6 rice paper sheets
1 cup (30g) snow pea or alfalfa
   sprouts
12 Thai basil leaves

DIPPING SAUCE
½ an avocado
2 tbsp Tamari/wheat free soy sauce
½ cup (75g) unsalted peanuts or
   other nut (optional)

Prep the prawns by removing the tails and making sure they are clean. Set aside.

Julienne the carrot and daikon using a peeler or finely slicing with a knife. Set aside.

Fill a large bowl with warm water and hydrate the rice paper sheets one at a time following packet instructions. Place the hydrated rice paper sheet on a damp tea towel and begin adding the fillings on one side of the sheet, starting with the sprouts and basil leaves and layering prawns, carrot and daikon. Roll the rice paper sheet up to form a roll, folding the sides in and securing with a dab of water if needed.

Prepare the dipping sauce by blitzing the avocado until smooth in a food processor or by using an immersion blender. Stir through the Tamari, starting with 1 tbsp and adding more according to desired taste. Roughly chop the peanuts and place in a bowl next to the dipping sauce.

CUCUMBER + QUINOA SUSHI ROLLS

These make great mid-morning snacks or served alongside a salad for lunch. Unlike traditional sushi rolls there's no white rice or sugary vinegar holding the whole thing together, just bite-size pieces of fresh, creamy goodness.

MAKES 6

1 long cucumber
8 tbsp hummus (page 68) or smashed
   avocado
⅔ cup (120g) cooked quinoa
Paprika for serving (optional)

Use a vegetable peeler to peel long strips the length of the cucumber. Depending on the width of the peeler you'll need 2-3 strips per sushi roll. Layer two strips of cucumber so they are just overlapping. Spread the hummus or smashed avocado the length of the cucumber strip and sprinkle over the cooked quinoa evenly. Beginning at one end, roll the cucumber up. Dust the top of each roll with paprika if desired.

ZUCCHINI, LEEK + RICOTTA FRITTATA

This is a great recipe to make on the weekend and then divide into portions for the week ahead. You can substitute cottage cheese or feta for the ricotta, and can use any vegetables you have on hand. Serve on its own or with a side salad, with a stack of these sitting in the fridge you'll never be left wondering what's for lunch again!

SERVES 4

1 tbsp extra virgin olive oil
2 garlic cloves, minced
2 zucchinis/courgettes, diced
2 leeks, white part only, thinly sliced
8 free range eggs
Handful of fresh parsley, finely chopped
150g/5 oz ricotta
Sea salt and black pepper to taste

Pre-heat the oven to 200°C/400°F.
In an ovenproof pan over a medium heat, add the oil and sweat the garlic, zucchini and leek for approximately 10 minutes.
In a bowl whisk the eggs and parsley together before folding in the ricotta. Add salt and pepper if desired.
Remove the pan from the heat and add the egg mixture, taking care to spread it evenly around the zucchini and leek. Place the pan in the oven and cook for 15 minutes until the frittata is golden brown.
Remove the frittata from the oven, slice and serve with a salad of choice.

HERBED MUSHROOMS ON SOCCA

Chickpea flour is a great staple to have on hand in the pantry for when you feel like a crispy, gluten free bread-pancake hybrid to top with delicious vegetables, or even to dip into a soup or curry sauce. Socca flatbread is simple to make and oh so delicious, add a combination of spices or herbs to the base recipe to adjust the flavour.

SERVES 4

SOCCA
1 cup (130g) chickpea flour/besan flour
1 cup (250ml) filtered water
1 tsp sea salt
2 tbsp extra virgin olive oil, plus more for the pan

HERBED MUSHROOMS
600g/1.3 lb mixed mushrooms, any variety
1 cup (40g) fresh flat leaf parsley, finely chopped
1 cup (50g) fresh dill, finely chopped
Juice from 1 lemon
Sea salt and black pepper

Prepare the socca by whisking the flour, water, salt and oil together in a bowl and letting it sit for ½ hour to allow the flour to absorb the moisture.
Slice the mushrooms and add to a hot pan with 1 tbsp of extra virgin olive oil. Cook on medium until the mushrooms have softened and reduced in size. Take the pan off the heat and stir through the parsley, dill, lemon juice, a good pinch of sea salt and pepper. Taste and adjust seasoning if needed.
Heat the grill/broiler in your oven and place a cast iron pan or an oven and stovetop safe dish/pan under the heat for 5 minutes. Carefully remove the pan using oven gloves, add a small amount of olive oil, just enough to coat the pan when you tilt it, then ladle in the batter and spread it around to form a thin layer. Place the pan back under the grill to cook for 5 minutes or until the bread turns a lovely golden brown. Remove from the oven and check the underside of the socca using a spatula, you may need to flip it over and cook the other side for a couple of minutes or it may be okay.
Serve the socca with the herbed mushrooms piled on top and additional fresh lemon juice if desired.

RICOTTA GNOCCHI WITH PAN SEARED SALMON + FENNEL

Salmon is a great source of Omega 3 fatty acids, said to be beneficial for supporting cell health and improving insulin sensitivity. Wild salmon is a much better choice than farmed salmon, which can contain high levels of antibiotics and Polychlorinated Biphenyl toxins (PCBs). While salmon may seem like an expensive addition to your shopping list, consider spending a bit more on better quality fish and reducing the amount and frequency you eat.

SERVES 2

RICOTTA GNOCCHI
1 free range egg yolk
1 tsp sea salt
250g/9 oz fresh, soft ricotta
½ cup (55g) brown rice flour (plus more for dusting)
Parmesan cheese (optional)

1 fennel bulb
1 tbsp unsalted butter or olive oil
1 large salmon fillet
1 tsp sea salt
1 tsp black pepper
Zest of 1 lemon
Extra virgin olive oil
1 cup (40g) peas
¼ cup (10g) fresh dill

In a small bowl, whisk the egg yolk and salt before folding in the ricotta. Using a spoon, slowly stir in the flour and Parmesan, if using, being careful not to overwork the mixture.

Sprinkle some flour on your work surface and working with a handful of the dough at a time, gently roll, starting from the middle and working out until you have a long sausage. If the mixture gets stuck on the work surface simply sprinkle a little more flour over it. Use a knife to cut the sausage into segments and place on a board or tray lined with baking paper. Repeat with the remaining dough.

Finely slice the fennel using a mandolin. Heat a pan with the butter or olive oil and add the fennel, sweat until tender, drain from the pan and set aside.

Season the salmon with sea salt, black pepper and lemon zest. Drizzle with extra virgin olive oil, heat a pan over medium and cook the fillet skin side down for 4 minutes each side. While the salmon is cooking steam the peas. Roughly shred the salmon in the pan with a fork.

Bring a large pot of salted water to the boil and cook the gnocchi; they will rise to the top when ready. Drain the gnocchi from the water and add to the pan of salmon with ¼ cup (60ml) of the pasta water.

Add the peas and fennel to the pan with the dill and additional fresh lemon juice or zest if desired. Gently stir the gnocchi through and serve.

Once you master this basic gnocchi recipe you can experiment with different flavours not only in the sauce but with the gnocchi itself. Try adding pureed pumpkin or sweet potato to the mix, reducing the amount of ricotta used to achieve the same texture. Season the gnocchi with different herbs and spices to suit your sauce such as cumin, paprika or even chilli.

SWEET POTATO, BLACK BEAN + JALAPENO BURGER PATTIES

Make these patties ahead of time and freeze individual portions for easy access. Add to a salad for lunch or go for the full burger, whether in a bun or lettuce leaves for a wheat free version. You can omit the jalapeno and replace with different spices, such as cumin or garam masala for a different taste.

MAKES 10

2 large sweet potatoes
1 cup (180g) cooked quinoa
1 cup (170g) cooked black beans
½ brown onion, diced
½ cup (20g) coriander/cilantro leaves,
  finely chopped
2 jalapñeo peppers, finely chopped
1 tbsp smoked paprika
1 tsp ground cumin
Pinch of salt and pepper

Preheat the oven to 180°C/350°F and line an oven tray with baking paper. Cut the sweet potatoes in half, drizzle with olive oil and a pinch of sea salt and roast for 40 minutes or until tender. Set aside to cool then scoop the soft flesh into a bowl and mash with a fork.

Thoroughly rinse the quinoa under water to remove any bitterness then add to a pan with 2 cups (500ml) of water and a pinch of salt over a medium heat. Cook until the quinoa has absorbed the water, about 15 minutes, then fluff with a fork and set aside to cool.

Add the cooked quinoa, the black beans, onion, coriander, jalapeño peppers, smoked paprika, cumin and a good pinch of sea salt and black pepper to the bowl of sweet potato. Mix together until all ingredients and spices are evenly distributed.

Line an oven tray with fresh baking paper. Form the mixture into even-sized balls then place on the tray and push down to flatten each into a burger pattie shape. Bake for 30 minutes or until crisp, flipping the patties over halfway through.

MUSTARD BEEF KEBABS

We often assume tasty food has to be complicated, with a long list of ingredients we need to do a special shopping trip to acquire. When you get back to basics and invest in quality produce, you can let the natural flavours of your ingredients shine through, without dousing them in sauces and marinades. These simple beef kebabs use good quality beef, bought fresh from the butcher and cooked on the same day. The simple marinade paired with the kebabs merely accentuates the flavour of the meat and doesn't try to compete with it. This marinade would also work wonderfully with chicken.

SERVES 2

400-500g/14-18 oz beef eye fillet
2 tbsp mustard of choice
2 tbsp extra virgin olive oil
2 garlic cloves, minced
Sea salt and black pepper

Preheat a barbecue or a grill plate while you prepare the kebabs. Remove any visible fat from the edge of the beef. Cube the eye fillet into an even number of chunks.

Use two metal or wooden skewers (soak wooden skewers overnight in water to prevent burning) and thread the beef onto each. Keep the meat pushed close together. You can add additional ingredients to the kebab if you choose, such as slices of onion or red capsicum (pepper).

Prepare the marinade by whisking together the mustard, extra virgin olive oil, minced garlic, sea salt and black pepper. Brush each kebab with the marinade until all used up.

By now the barbecue or grill plate should be hot. Cook the kebabs for 3-4 minutes each side then remove and set aside to rest for 5 minutes.

Serve with a side salad and an optional squeeze of fresh lemon juice over the beef.

PULLED CIDER PORK WITH ROASTED GARLIC + APPLE SALAD

This is a great dish to share with a group of people and really only needs a little preparation the night before cooking. Many recipes use apple cider to marinate the pork in before cooking but to avoid those high amounts of sugar this recipe uses apple cider vinegar with a touch of raw honey to add sweetness.

SERVES 6

PULLED PORK

1.5kg/3.3 lb boneless pork shoulder
½ cup (125ml) apple cider vinegar
1 cup (250ml) chicken stock (page 79)
2 garlic cloves, minced
1 tbsp sea salt
¼ cup (60ml) raw honey
1 tsp mustard seeds
1½ tbsp smoked paprika
2 tsp sea salt

ROASTED GARLIC + APPLE SALAD

1 garlic bulb
2 green apples
¼ cup (60ml) lemon juice
250g/9 oz salad greens, such as baby spinach, rocket/arugula, watercress
2 tbsp extra virgin olive oil

Place the pork in a large plastic ziplock bag or in a large bowl.

In a bowl, combine the apple cider vinegar, chicken stock, garlic, salt and honey, whisk until combined.

In a small, dry pan toast the mustard seeds for 2 minutes until they begin to pop. Add the mustard seeds to the cider vinegar mixture and stir through. Pour the marinade over the pork shoulder. If using a bag, seal the bag and massage the marinade around the meat. If using a bowl, turn the pork over a couple of times in the liquid before resting it flesh (not skin) side down and covering the bowl with plastic wrap. Place in the fridge overnight.

Remove the pork from the fridge at least half an hour before putting it on to cook. Mix the smoked

paprika and sea salt together then rub over the flesh side of the pork (not the skin).

To cook the pork you can use a pressure cooker (cooking time 2-2.5 hours on high) with some of the marinade liquid at the bottom of the bowl, a cast iron pot in the oven (heat the oven to 160°C/320°F and cook low and slow, for approximately 4 hours with a little of the liquid in the bottom of the pan), or on a BBQ (4-5 hours).

To test if the pork is ready, use two forks to shred some of the meat, if it comes off easily the muscle meat has broken down enough and you can set the meat aside to shred, discard the skin. If it is still tough, cook for a further 30 minutes and check again.

Prepare the salad by preheating the oven to 180°C/350°F and lining an oven tray with baking paper. Cut the top off the garlic bulb and place the bulb on the tray, drizzle with a little olive oil and roast for 20-30 minutes until the cloves are soft and beginning to caramelise. Remove from the oven and set aside to cool.

Core the apples and finely slice, either into crescents or matchsticks. Lightly coat the apple in lemon juice to stop it from browning.

In a bowl combine the salad leaves, roasted garlic and apple slices then drizzle the extra virgin olive oil over the top and serve alongside the pulled pork.

INSTANT NOODLE POTS

Quick noodles with flavour sachets are a popular meal option for many people as they're cheap and flavourful. They're also usually jam-packed with high levels of salt and artificial ingredients. Making instant noodle pots for home, school or the office is incredibly easy and much healthier than the store-bought variety.

SPRING VEGETABLE

SERVES 1

½ carrot, grated
½ cup (65g) frozen peas
1 celery stick, diced
1 spring onion/scallion, diced
1 tsp ground cumin
½ tsp curry powder
1 tsp sea salt
50g/1.8 oz brown rice vermicelli
  noodles
1 cup (250ml) boiling water

Add the carrot, peas, celery, spring onion, cumin, curry powder and sea salt in a glass jar. Place the lid on and shake to combine the flavours. Remove the lid, add the noodles and reseal the jar. When ready to eat, pour in the boiling water until the contents are just covered. Let the jar sit for 2 minutes for the noodles to soften and the vegetables to heat through.

CREAMY MUSHROOM

SERVES 1

⅓ cup (80ml) coconut milk
1 bok choy bulb
Handful of oyster mushrooms
Handful of dried porcini mushrooms
1 tsp garam masala
1 tsp sea salt
50g/1.8 oz brown rice vermicelli
  noodles
1 cup (250ml) boiling water

Pour the coconut milk into the bottom of a glass jar. Finely slice the bok choy and oyster mushrooms and add to the jar followed by the dried porcini mushrooms. Dust over the garam masala and sea salt then add the noodles to the top and fasten the lid. When ready to eat, pour in the boiling water, wait 2 minutes and then stir the contents of the jar together.

OODLES OF ZOODLES

For those wanting wheat-free pasta options that don't come from a packet, investing in a spiraliser opens up a world of noodle options. The most common vegetable to turn into noodles is without doubt the zucchini/courgette. Known as zoodles or courgetti, one zucchini transforms into a generous bowl of noodles for one person. Pair your zoodles with a sauce of choice and enjoy!

VEG PACKED BOLOGNAISE

SERVES 4

1 brown onion
4 garlic cloves
400g/14 oz minced beef
1 large carrot
200g/7 oz pumpkin, any variety
1 zucchini/courgette
2 celery stalks
1 can of crushed tomatoes
1 tbsp dried basil
2 tbsp red wine or red wine vinegar
Sea salt and black pepper

Finely dice the brown onion, crush the garlic and add to a large pan with a drizzle of extra virgin olive oil. Cook over a medium heat until the onion softens then add the minced beef and cook until browned.

Grate the carrot, pumpkin and zucchini and add to the pot. Finely dice the celery and add to the pot, stir so that all the vegetables are mixed with the meat. Add the tomatoes then fill the can with water and pour into the pot. Add the dried basil, red wine and a good pinch of sea salt and ground black pepper. Stir to combine then reduce the heat to low and let the sauce simmer for 45 minutes.

CURRIED EGG ZOODLE SALAD

SERVES 1

1 zucchini/courgette
2 free range eggs
1 tbsp hulled tahini
1 tsp curry powder
Handful of chives, finely chopped
Pinch of sea salt and ground black pepper

Prepare the zoodles using your spiraliser, steam for 2-3 minutes until just tender and set aside.

Place the eggs in a small saucepan and cover with cold water. Bring to the boil and cook to your liking (2 minutes for a soft boiled egg, 4-5 minutes for medium boiled, depending on the size of the eggs). Once the eggs have cooled, peel the shell off and roughly chop.

Add the tahini, curry powder, chives, sea salt and black pepper to the eggs, stir to combine then taste and adjust seasoning if required. Stir the curried egg gently through the zoodles and serve.

CHUNKY GUACAMOLE ZOODLE SALAD

All the flavours of a great guacamole but with added texture, stirred through fresh zucchini noodles and served chilled on its own or alongside vegetables or meat makes a fantastic meal.

SERVES 4

2 large zucchinis (courgettes)
2 large avocados, any variety
12 cherry/small tomatoes
12 bocconcini/baby Mozzarella balls
1 cup (25g) fresh coriander/cilantro leaves
Juice of 1 lemon

Prepare the zoodles by spiralising the zucchinis and setting aside. You can eat the zoodles raw or lightly steam them for a tenderer noodle. If steaming, let the noodles cool before stirring the chunky guacamole through.

Halve the avocados, remove the pits and scoop the flesh out. Cut the avocado into chunks and add to a large serving bowl.

Slice the tomatoes and bocconcini balls in half and add to the bowl. Roughly chop the coriander leaves and add to the bowl.

Pour the lemon juice over the avocado, tomatoes, bocconcini and coriander and season with a pinch of salt. Add the zoodles to the bowl and gently mix through using tongs.

CAULIFLOWER CARBONARA

Carbonara is such a treat, a real winter warmer or comfort dish thanks to the combination of eggs, milk and cheese. While the real-deal is okay occasionally, for a more frequent warming feast try this cauliflower substitute.

SERVES 2

6 bacon rashers, any cut
1 head of cauliflower
1 small onion
2 garlic cloves
½ cup (45g) finely shaved Parmesan cheese
Sea salt and black pepper

Preheat the oven to 180°C/350°F and line an oven tray with baking paper. Spread the bacon in a single layer over the tray and bake for 20 minutes or until the bacon is crispy. Set aside to cool then place the bacon in the bowl of a food processor fitted with an S blade and pulse until the bacon forms a fine crumb.

Remove the cauliflower florets from the stem and steam, either using a microwave or a steamer basket on the stovetop over simmering water. Once steamed tender, puree the cauliflower using an immersion blender and set aside.

Finely dice the onion and mince the garlic, add to a pan over medium heat. Cook until the onion is softened, about 5 minutes, then add the cauliflower puree and heat through. Remove the pan from the heat and stir through the shaved Parmesan cheese with a good pinch of sea salt and ground black pepper. Taste and adjust seasoning if needed. Serve the carbonara sauce with the bacon crumb over the top.

REVIVING GREEN PESTO

Pairing this fresh green pesto with the zoodles is a super green meal, tasty and rejuvenating.

SERVES 2

Handful of fresh flatleaf parsley leaves
Handful of fresh coriander/cilantro leaves
1 red chilli
Juice of 1 lemon
1 tsbp apple cider vinegar
Water as needed

Combine the parsley, coriander, chilli, lemon juice and apple cider vinegar in the bowl of a food processor or blender. Add a small amount of water in as needed to help make a dressing-like consistency. Alternatively you could use a drizzle of good-quality extra virgin olive oil. Heat the zoodles then stir through the pesto directly before serving.

SWEET POTATO NOODLE STIR-FRY

Try spiralising different vegetables, such as sweet potatoes, which give a sturdy noodle ideal for using in stir-fries. Prep all of your ingredients before you begin cooking, heat the wok up and you'll have a meal ready in minutes, it really is a quicker and healthier option to fast food.

SERVES 1

1 medium sweet potato
3 large mushrooms, any variety
1½ cups (100g) kale or other leafy
  green
1 spring onion/scallion
1 free range egg
1 tbsp Tamari/wheat free soy sauce
1 tsp black pepper

Peel the sweet potato, spiralise into noodles and set aside.
  Roughly chop the mushrooms, kale and spring onion and set aside.
  Crack the egg and lightly whisk it.

Heat up a wok with 1 tbsp of coconut oil. Add the egg, mushrooms, kale and spring onion and cook for 30 seconds, stirring with a wooden spoon or spatula. Add the sweet potato noodles, the Tamari and black pepper. Cook for 2-3 minutes, adding a dash of water if needed to keep the mixture loose from the wok.
  You can pre-steam the sweet potato noodles before adding them to the wok if you would prefer a tenderer noodle, while adding it straight to the wok will help the noodles retain their shape and texture.

Real Food Gathering

Weekends are a great time to get together with family or friends and share a special meal. We can afford to slow down, unwind and spend more time walking the farmers' market or shops, carefully selecting what we'll cook. Choosing the right menu doesn't have to be complicated, and creating delicious and healthy dishes doesn't need to take all day. Whether you're flying solo in the kitchen or you have an extra pair of hands to help, the following menu is hassle free and on the table by lunchtime.

HERBED CAULIFLOWER RICE SALAD

Riced cauliflower is an excellent alternative to traditional rice salad or cous cous and when tossed with delicious fresh herbs some people may even struggle to tell the difference. Having a food processor makes this recipe a lot easier, or at least quicker, to make, however you can rice cauliflower by hand with some keen knife skills, a large chopping board and some patience. Customise the herbs to your liking or what's in season.

SERVES 6

1 head of cauliflower
2 tbsp mustard seeds
1½ tbsp cumin seeds
1 cup (40g) fresh coriander/cilantro
  leaves
½ cup (20g) fresh parsley leaves
⅓ cup (80ml) fresh lemon juice
Sea salt and black pepper to taste

Remove the cauliflower stalk and trim the florets off. Add the cauliflower to the bowl of a food processor and pulse until a fine crumb forms, it's better to have some chunks in there for texture than to blitz it too much. Add the riced cauliflower to a large bowl and set aside.

In a dry pan over a low heat, add the mustard and cumin seeds and toast until they begin to pop and become fragrant, up to 5 minutes.

Finely chop the coriander and parsley then stir through the cauli-flower rice along with the mustard and cumin seeds. Season the salad with fresh lemon juice, sea salt and black pepper.

WATERCRESS + CHIVE SOUP

Watercress has a natural pepper flavour that works so well in soup. You can serve this dish in the warmer or cooler months and simply adjust the thickness to suit the weather. For cooler days transitioning into winter, add an extra couple of potatoes to the stock to help thicken it up. For warmer months you may choose to omit the potatoes altogether for a lighter and thinner soup.

SERVES 6

8 cups (2L) vegetable stock
4 medium potatoes
1 bunch of chives
1 bunch of fresh watercress
Sea salt to taste

Add the stock to a saucepan and bring to a simmer over medium heat.

Peel the potatoes and dice into even, small cubes. Either steam the potatoes separately to speed the process up or add them to the stock to cook until tender.

Finely dice the chives and add to the stock, cook for 5 minutes.

Once the potatoes are tender, puree the mixture until smooth using a blender or handheld immersion blender. Return the pot to the stove over low heat.

Finely chop the watercress, discarding any hard stalks. Add the watercress to the soup and cook for 2 minutes before removing the pot from the heat. Blitz the soup again until smooth. You can eat as is or stir through ½ cup (125ml) of coconut milk for added creaminess.

Make salads + vegetables the centre of your meal and build around those with meat + extras

MEATBALLS IN SIMPLE TOMATO SAUCE

Meatballs are always a hit, whether served in a traditional tomato sauce or something a bit different, they're easy and quick to make, and disappear off the plate even faster. These meatballs are free from breadcrumbs or other binders, such as almond meal. This makes them more delicate and prone to falling apart, which is why they're gently cooked in the sauce, to avoid handling. The end result is a moist and flavourful meatball.

SERVES 4-6

TOMATO SAUCE

1 brown onion, diced
2 garlic cloves, minced
2 tbsp Worcestershire sauce
2 tbsp tomato paste
8 fresh tomatoes, diced
Sea salt and black pepper

MEATBALLS

250g/9 oz beef mince
250g/9 oz lamb mince
2 tbsp dried basil
1 tbsp smoked paprika
Fresh parsley, to serve
Parmesan cheese, to serve
    (optional)

In a large pan over high heat, add a drizzle of extra virgin olive oil and cook onion and garlic until softened and fragrant.

Add the Worcestershire sauce, tomato paste and diced tomatoes to the pan. Stir through a good pinch of sea salt and a grinding of black pepper.

Reduce the heat to low and let the sauce simmer for 30 minutes.

Make the meatballs by mixing the beef and lamb mince together with the dried basil. Take handfuls of the mixture and roll between your hands into balls. Keep the balls small to medium so they don't break apart when you put them in the sauce. Gently place the meatballs into the large pot of sauce and use a wooden spoon to carefully stir the mixture so the balls are covered with sauce. As there are no breadcrumbs or egg in the meatballs to help keep them together, it's important to take care with this step.

Cook the meatballs in the simmering tomato sauce for 20 minutes or until cooked through. Test one meatball before serving. Serve the meatballs with freshly chopped parsley and Parmesan cheese if using.

CARAMELISED HONEY + SOY MEATBALLS

Meatballs are a great mid-week meal to whip up but can easily be transformed into something special for the weekend by playing around with simple seasonings that deliver a tonne of flavour. Opt for a mixture of beef and pork minces rather than simply beef; the added flavour is well worth it. You can make these ahead of time and freeze raw, then simply defrost in the fridge the night before cooking.

MAKES 12

500g/1.1 lb mixture of ground beef
    and pork mince
1 brown onion, diced

2 garlic cloves, crushed
2 tbsp raw honey
⅓ cup (80ml) apple cider vinegar
⅓ cup (80ml) Tamari/wheat free
    soy sauce)
½ cup (30g) sourdough breadcrumbs
    (almond meal for wheat free)
1-2 free range eggs

Preheat the oven to 180°C/350°F and line an oven tray with baking paper.

Add the mince, onion and garlic to a large bowl and set aside.

In a small pan on the stovetop, combine the honey, apple cider vinegar and Tamari. Cook over a low heat until the mixture has thickened, about 10-15 minutes. Set aside to cool for 5 minutes then pour half into the meatball mixture and set the other half aside for later.

Add the breadcrumbs and egg to the bowl and use your hands to mix until all the ingredients are combined. Start with one egg and add another if the mixture feels too dry. If the mixture is too wet, add some more breadcrumbs. You should be able to easily roll the mixture into balls that hold their shape but remain soft.

Place the meatballs on the lined oven tray, evenly spaced apart. Rather than cook the meatballs in oil, baking them helps further caramelise the honey and Tamari in the seasoning. Bake the meatballs for 20-30 minutes until cooked through.

Before serving, return the pan with the remaining honey mixture in it to the stovetop and gently heat on low until the sauce is warm. Drizzle the extra sauce over the meatballs and serve on top of fresh greens.

CARROT + BLACK SESAME SALAD

I feel like carrots often don't make the cut when it comes to salads. We'll happily steam them and eat alongside a piece of meat, or chop them raw and eat as a snack, but a hard chunk of carrot in a salad is not a desirable morsel. This recipe will transform the way you think of a carrot salad. It's incredibly easy and quick to prepare, with minimal dressing and fuss; this is one of the best examples of how Real Food can shine.

SERVES 6

2 large orange carrots
2 large yellow carrots
100g/3.5 oz good quality goat
    cheese (marinated in extra virgin
    olive oil if possible)
¼ cup (35g) black sesame seeds

Peel the carrots and trim the tough ends. Using a julienne peeler, slice the carrots into thin strands. A julienne peeler is a cheap addition to your kitchen but is not a necessity. You can finely slice the carrot with a knife but this will of course take longer and may yield different results.

Add the carrots to a serving bowl or platter, piled high. Dot the salad with chunks of goat cheese and drizzle some of the marinating oil over the salad. If the goat cheese you are using didn't come in oil, simply drizzle some extra virgin olive oil from your cupboard over the top.

Sprinkle the black sesame seeds over the top of the salad and serve. If you can't locate black sesame seeds you can replace with regular sesame seeds, which should be available at all supermarkets.

CHOOSE YOUR GREENS SALAD

Making a great green salad can often depend on what's in season and also what looks great when you go shopping. Often I have wanted to make a salad with fresh radish leaves only to be disappointed by the limp leaves looking back at me from the shelf. The best approach to making a green salad is to be open-minded and use what looks best and what's affordable. In summer lean more towards different lettuce varieties to bulk up your salad, in winter try Tuscan kale or bitter greens.

SERVES 6

450g/1 lb mixed greens of choice
1 large avocado
1 large cucumber

Thoroughly rinse and dry the greens and add to a large bowl. Slice the avocado and cucumber and add to the greens.

CHOOSE YOUR DRESSING

KEEP IT SIMPLE
Scatter freshly chopped dill and a handful of pepitas (pumpkin seeds) over the top then toss through. Drizzle olive oil over before serving.

SUPER GREENS
Puree ½ an avocado with the juice of 1 lemon, a good pinch of sea salt, and enough water to thin the dressing out to a pourable consistency. Drizzle over and toss through before serving.

BIT OF A BITE
Whisk together ¼ cup (60ml) of apple cider vinegar with 1 tbsp of rice wine vinegar and 2 crushed garlic cloves. Thin down with water to desired consistency and toss through the salad before serving.

SWEET SIDE
Whisk together 1 tbsp of hulled tahini with 1 tsbp of pomegranate molasses, thin down with water to a pourable consistency then toss through the salad before serving. For additional crunch and sweetness, add some pomegranate seeds on the top.

GINGER + LEMON THYME FIZZ

This sweet, natural alternative to soft drink and soda is a real crowd-pleaser. Refreshing in warmer months served with plenty of ice in chilled glasses, or served as the seasons drift into cooler temperatures, with the ginger providing some much-needed warmth; this fizz is a simple syrup that can be mixed with still or sparkling water.

SERVES 6

150g/5.3 oz fresh ginger root
2 tsbp raw honey
Large handful of fresh lemon thyme
   sprigs (up to 1 bunch)
1 cup (250ml) filtered water
Water or sparkling water to serve

Prepare the ginger by slicing it into even chunks. You can leave the skin on, however if there are any dirty-looking bits, remove those before adding to a small saucepan. Add the honey, lemon thyme sprigs and water, stir then leave to simmer for 30 minutes. Check the liquid level periodically, topping up if it is getting too low. You want the syrup to be concentrated but not too thick.

   Pour the syrup through a sieve into a jar or jug. When ready to serve, divide the syrup evenly between glasses and top up with still or sparkling water.

PUMPKIN + RASPBERRY SWIRL CAKE

This cake was so delicious that after I photographed it for this spread, one of my brother's chickens jumped up on the table and went to town, leaving us with only a couple of pieces of un-pecked cake to enjoy after our meal. The combination of pureed pumpkin and raspberries may seem a tad unusual but it's just one of those things that works – trust me!

SERVES 6-8 (OR 1 CHICKEN)

4 free range eggs
2 tbsp maple syrup
½ cup (125ml) coconut oil, melted
1½ tsp vanilla powder
1 tsp all spice
1½ cups (195g) brown rice flour
1½ cups (200g) almond meal
2 tsp baking powder
Pinch of sea salt
½ medium pumpkin, skin and seeds
  removed
1½ tsp ground cinnamon
1 cup (150g) raspberries, fresh
  or frozen

Preheat the oven to 180°C/350°F. Line a square or round cake tin with baking paper.

In a bowl whisk together the eggs, maple syrup, coconut oil, vanilla powder and all spice. Sift in the brown rice flour, almond meal, baking powder and sea salt. Stir until combined; it will be a thick batter. Use a spatula or the back of a spoon to smooth the batter down into the pan.

Dice the pumpkin and steam until tender, about 5 minutes. Puree the pumpkin with the cinnamon using an immersion blender. Pour the pumpkin mixture over the top of the batter, spreading evenly over the top.

Heat the raspberries with ¼ cup (60ml) of water for 2 minutes then puree until smooth using an immersion blender. Add dollops of the raspberry puree over the top of the pumpkin layer then use a skewer to swirl the raspberries gently through the pumpkin to create a pattern.

Bake in the oven for 45 minutes or until an inserted skewer comes out clean.

Not every meal should end on a sweet note but on weekends, when surrounded by family or friends, a slice of cake or sweet treat can be best enjoyed!

Something sweet

CARAMEL STUFFED DOUBLE NUT CRUNCHES

These are the perfect balance of savoury and sweet, with the nutty cookies seamlessly complimenting the sticky, sweet date caramel and making it hard to stop at one. What makes these cookies even more tempting is the short list of ingredients, which most people have on hand in the fridge and cupboard, plus the caramel can be made ahead of time and stored in an airtight container in the fridge for up to 2 weeks, in case you're struck by a craving unexpectantly.

MAKES 8

1 cup (135g) smooth nut butter
  of choice
1 free range egg
⅓ cup (80ml) rice malt syrup
  or sweetener of choice
⅔ cup (80g) crushed walnuts
1 tsp ground cinnamon
Sea salt

CARAMEL FILLING
6 Medjool dates, pitted
1 tsp vanilla powder
1 tbsp coconut oil
Pinch of sea salt

Preheat the oven to 180°C/350°F.

In a bowl, stir the nut butter, egg, rice malt syrup, walnuts and cinnamon together. Take spoonfuls of the mixture and roll into balls.

Place on an oven tray lined with baking paper and press down with a fork. Sprinkle the tops of each cookie with a pinch of sea salt. Bake in the oven for 10 minutes.

Prepare the caramel filling by soaking the dates in boiling water for 10 minutes. Drain then add the pitted dates to the bowl of a food processor with the vanilla powder, coconut oil and sea salt. Blitz until a smooth caramel-coloured mixture comes together.

Sandwich two cookies together with a generous spoonful of the caramel filling and store in an air-tight container. Any leftover caramel filling can be stored in the fridge for up to two weeks.

BAKED GINGERBREAD DOUGHNUTS WITH TAHINI GLAZE

Baked doughnuts are a revelation in home cooked delights. Of course they'll never be as mouth watering as the deep fried versions but these can be enjoyed more regularly without having to undo the top button on your pants afterwards. Pairing gingerbread with a tahini glaze may sound a little strange to some people but it is worth trying at least once. The spiciness of the gingerbread is mellowed by the nutty tahini and it's surprising how well they compliment each other.

MAKES 8

1 cup (130g) brown rice flour
1 tsp baking powder
½ tsp ground cinnamon
1½ tsp ground ginger
Pinch of sea salt
1 tbsp coconut oil, melted
1 free range egg
2 tbsp milk
1 tsp molasses
1 tbsp maple or rice malt syrup

TAHINI GLAZE
½ cup (115g) hulled tahini
1 tbsp maple syrup
Pinch of sea salt

Preheat the oven to 180°C/350°F.

Sift the rice flour, baking powder, cinnamon, ginger and sea salt into a bowl.

In a separate bowl whisk the coconut oil, egg, milk, molasses and maple syrup together then stir through the flour mix. Transfer the batter to a piping bag (or use a ziplock bag and snip the end off) and pipe the mixture into 6 holes of a doughnut pan, careful not to overfill the holes as the batter will rise considerably.

Bake the doughnuts in the oven for 15-20 minutes until golden brown, the doughnuts should feel light and an inserted skewer should come out clean. Remove the doughnuts from the pan and cool on a wire rack.

Prepare the glaze by adding the tahini, maple syrup and sea salt to a bowl and whisking until smooth, adding a dash of water if the glaze needs thinning out.

Once the doughnuts have cooled down, spread 1 tbsp of glaze onto each and enjoy. Store any leftovers in an airtight container to be eaten within 2 days.

GOJI BERRY + SEA SALT TRUFFLES

Heaven is surely an unlimited supply of raw chocolate truffles while you lounge about on a fluffy cloud. These truffles are not only quick to make but basically foolproof, meaning you throw everything together in a bowl, stick it in the fridge to harden, then roll into bite-size treats that dreams are made of.

MAKES 12

4 tbsp cacao butter
3 tbsp coconut oil
3 tbsp rice malt syrup, honey
  or maple syrup
¾ cup (90g) raw cacao powder
1 tsp sea salt
½ cup (55g) goji berries

COATING
⅓ cup (40g) goji berries
¼ cup (20g) unsweetened shredded
  coconut

In a small saucepan melt the cacao butter and coconut oil over a low heat. As soon as the mixture turns liquid remove it from the heat and whisk in your sweetener of choice.

Sift in the raw cacao powder and whisk until the mixture is smooth and glossy.

Stir through the sea salt and goji berries then pour the mixture into a shallow bowl and place in the refrigerator for 15-20 minutes.

While the mixture is cooling, prepare the coating to roll the truffles in. Place the goji berries and coconut in the bowl of a food processor and blitz into a powder. Pour the powder over a large plate and set aside.

When the chocolate mixture has begun to harden, take it out of the fridge and use a teaspoon to scoop up small amounts. Roll the chocolate between your palms into a ball shape, working quickly as your body heat will melt the mixture.

Place the balls on the plate of goji berry powder, roll to coat the outside then place the truffles in an airtight container and store in the refrigerator for up to 2 weeks.

TRY:

COFFEE + COCONUT
Mix 1 heaped tbsp of coffee granules into the basic truffle mixture (omitting the sea salt and goji berries from the previous recipe) and roll the balls in unsweetened shredded coconut.

BLUEBERRY + GINGER
Mix 1 heaped tbsp of freshly grated ginger and ⅓ cup (50g) of blueberries into the basic truffle mixture and roll the balls in raw cacao powder.

COOKIES + CREAM CRUNCH
Mix ½ cup (75g) buckinis with 1 tbsp of raw cacao powder and 1 tbsp of melted coconut oil. Stir the chocolate buckinis through the basic truffle mixture and roll into balls.

For the cream coating, mix 1 cup (250ml) of coconut butter with 1 cup (250ml) of coconut oil, ⅓ cup (80ml) of rice malt syrup or maple syrup and ½ tsp of vanilla powder in a small pan.

Once smooth, gently insert a fork or skewer into each truffle and dip into the mixture, turning to let any excess run off. Place the truffles on a plate lined with baking paper and place in the fridge to set. Store any leftover coconut butter mixture in an airtight container or freeze for next time.

RAW CARROT CAKE SLICE

Carrot cake is one of those desserts that sounds healthy but is often far from it. Here we replace refined white flour with rolled oats or quinoa flakes, sweeten with dates instead of white sugar, and top the cake off with an indulgent coconut butter frosting instead of cream cheese. The earthy flavour of the raw carrots still shines through and is not masked by the other ingredients, making this a real treat for those who love the taste of their vegetables.

SERVES 8

6 Medjool dates, pitted
3 large carrots, peeled
1 cup (100g) rolled oats or quinoa
   flakes
½ cup (85g) pecans
¾ cup (60g) unsweetened shredded
   coconut
1 tsp ground cinnamon
½ tsp ground nutmeg

FROSTING
1 cup (230g) coconut butter
1 cup (250ml) melted coconut oil
⅓ cup (80ml) rice malt syrup
   or maple syrup
Vanilla powder and extra pecans
   for decorating

Soak the dates in a bowl of boiling water while you prepare the cake mixture.

Peel the carrots and chop into small chunks. Place in the bowl of a food processor along with the oats, pecans, coconut, cinnamon and nutmeg. Blitz until the mixture forms a fine crumb and the carrot is evenly distributed.

Drain the dates from the water and remove the pits. Place the dates in the bowl of the food processor and pulse the mixture until mixed with the carrot.

Line a rectangular or square baking tin with baking paper and press half of the carrot mixture into the tin, pushing it down firmly.

Prepare the frosting by adding the coconut butter, coconut oil and sweetener of choice to the bowl of a food processor and blitzing until smooth.

Spread ⅓ of the frosting mixture over the carrot mixture in the tin, smooth out into each corner with a knife. Place in the refrigerator for 5 minutes for the frosting to harden.

Press the rest of the carrot cake mixture into the tin then spread the remaining coconut frosting over the top, sprinkle with a pinch of vanilla powder and a small handful of chopped pecans.

Set in the refrigerator for 20 minutes, slice into bars or squares and store in an airtight container in the fridge.

MACADAMIA ROCK CAKES

Consider making these in mini muffin tins or muffin liners for a bite-size treat. With a rich coconut flavour and a hit of raw chocolate on the top, these rock cakes are sure to curb any cravings you may encounter after dinner.

MAKES 6

1½ cups (225g) macadamia nuts
1 cup (80g) shredded coconut
3 tbsp coconut butter
1 tsp sea salt
¼ cup (60ml) rice malt syrup
¼ cup (60ml) coconut oil, melted
¼ cup (30g) raw cacao powder
Pinch of sea salt

Place the macadamia nuts in a food processor and pulse until crumbs form. Add the coconut, coconut butter, salt and rice malt syrup and pulse until combined. Press spoonfuls of the mixture into 6 holes of a muffin tin. Keep adding mixture until all used and press down hard. You can also make these in baking cups or using muffin liners. Place the tin in the refrigerator for 1 hour until the cakes have firmed up.

Prepare the chocolate topping by combining the coconut oil, raw cacao, sea salt and rice malt syrup. Stir or whisk until smooth.

Take the rock cakes out of the refrigerator and use a butter knife to help ease them out of the tin. Dip the top of each cake into the chocolate mixture and turn to drain the excess. Place on a plate ready to eat or store in the fridge.

RASPBERRY RIPE "CHEESECAKE"

Cheesecake is a personally favourite of mine and because I don't have it often I mostly use cream cheese when I am making it, but for those who are after a dairy-free cheesecake this recipe might tempt you. Soaking and blending nuts, such as cashews, to turn into vegan cheeses and butters is nothing new. You'll need a good blender or food processor to whizz the cashews up and ensure a smooth texture akin to cream cheese but the end result is just as satisfying as the traditional recipes.

SERVES 8-10

BASE
1 cup (170g) macadamia nuts
1 cup (80g) shredded unsweetened
   coconut
¼ cup (60ml) rice malt syrup or maple
   syrup
¼ cup (60ml) coconut oil, melted

FILLING
2 cups (250g) raw cashews, soaked
   in water overnight
½ cup (40g) shredded unsweetened
   coconut
½ cup (125ml) rice malt syrup
   or maple syrup
1 vanilla bean pod, seeds scraped
   out
¼ cup (60ml) coconut oil, melted
¼ cup (60ml) coconut milk
¼ tsp sea salt
1 cup (150g) raspberries, fresh
   or frozen

CHOCOLATE GANACHE
5 tbsp coconut oil
5 tbsp coconut milk
3 tbsp maple syrup
6 tbsp raw cacao powder

TO TOP
1 cup (150g) fresh raspberries

To make the base, add the macadamia nuts and coconut to the bowl of a food processor and mix on high until a crumb forms. Add the rice malt syrup and coconut oil and blitz until the mixture is combined and sticks together.

Line a baking tin (any shape) with baking paper and press the mixture into the tin, taking care to push it into the corners and create an even layer. Place the tin in the refrigerator for 30 minutes to set.

To make the filling, rinse the soaked cashews in fresh water, drain, then add to the bowl of a food processor along with the shredded coconut, rice malt syrup, vanilla seeds, coconut oil, coconut milk and sea salt. Mix on high until the filing is silky and smooth, stopping every now and then to scrape down the sides of the bowl. It's important to get the mixture as smooth as possible at this stage as it will guarantee a better texture when it comes to eating the cheesecake later.

Roughly chop the raspberries and gently fold through the filling. Pour the mixture on top of the base and place the tin in the freezer for 2 hours to set.

Prepare the chocolate ganache by melting coconut oil in a small saucepan and adding the coconut milk and maple syrup. Stir until combined then sift in the raw cacao powder and stir until combined and glossy. Transfer the mixture to a small bowl and refrigerate for 20 minutes until it begins to harden. Transfer the mixture to a piping bag and pipe rounds of the ganache over the top of the cake, or simply spread the ganache over the top with a knife.

When ready to serve, scatter the remaining raspberries over the top.

Slice the cheesecake while it's still firm but let the cake sit for 5-10 minutes before serving to allow it to soften slightly.

Take the base cashew "cheesecake" recipe, play around with different flavours + have some fun. Try pureeing blueberries + blackberries into the mixture for a delightful purple treat or go for a sweet + savoury combo by blitzing avocado with raw cacao + a sweetener of choice for a different topping.

ZUCCHINI + BLUEBERRY TEA CAKE

This barely sweet tea cake earns its name because it goes perfectly with a freshly brewed cup of tea. The addition of zucchini keeps the cake moist while the blueberries deliver pockets of sweetness and tartness, while also giving the cake a beautiful colour. I love to eat this fresh from the oven, warm with a smear of soft grass fed butter.

SERVES 8

3 free range eggs
1 cup (250ml) coconut oil, melted
½ cup (125ml) milk of choice
½ cup (125ml) rice malt syrup
  or sweetener of choice
1 tsp vanilla powder
1 large zucchini/courgette
1½ cups (195g) brown rice flour
1 cup (120g) buckwheat flour
2 tsp baking powder
Pinch of sea salt
200g/7 oz blueberries, fresh
  or frozen

Preheat the oven to 180°C/350°F and line a loaf tin with baking paper.

In a medium bowl whisk the eggs with the melted coconut oil, milk, sweetener and vanilla powder. Grate the zucchini and add to the wet mixture, stir until combined.

Sift in the rice and buckwheat flours along with the baking powder and salt. Fold through the blueberries then pour the batter into the lined loaf tin. Bake in the oven for 40 minutes or until an inserted skewer comes out clean.

Remove from the pan and let the cake rest on a wire rack for 10 minutes. Serve warm or cold with a smear of coconut honey butter (page 61) or grass fed butter.

CHAI TEA POACHED PEACHES WITH MACADAMIA CRUMBLE

You can make one large crumble with this recipe or serve in individual pots, which works great for a party. The poached peaches can be served warm or chilled, depending on the occasion. These are great to make ahead of time and store in the refrigerator for up to three days, and of course the peaches can be substituted with any stone fruit of choice.

SERVES 6

2 tbsp loose chai tea leaves/mix
6 cups (1.5L) filtered water
6 peaches
1 cup (150g) macadamia nuts
½ cup (40g) unsweetened shredded coconut
25g/1 oz grass fed butter
1 tsp ground cinnamon

Add the tea and water to a saucepan over medium heat and let it simmer for 5 minutes to brew.

Cut a cross into the top of each peach then lower them gently into the water. If the water doesn't cover the peaches, top the pan up with a little extra water. Poach the peaches in the tea for 30 minutes until tender then remove the pan from the heat and place in the fridge for anywhere from 1 hour to overnight to let the flavour intensify.

Peel the skin off the peaches and cut or pull the peaches into chunks. Evenly distribute the peaches between jars or bowls and prepare the macadamia crumble.

Preheat the oven to 180°C/350°F. In the bowl of a food processor fitted with an S blade blitz the macadamia nuts, coconut, butter and cinnamon until a crumb forms. Spread the crumb over an oven tray lined with baking paper and bake for 15 minutes or until the mixture has browned.

Sprinkle the macadamia crumble over the top of the poached peaches and serve.

Poaching the fruit in tea removes the need for adding sweetener to the recipe and allows you to infuse a range of flavours into the peaches. Try experimenting with different tea and fruit combinations. If you cannot source loose leaf tea, simply use tea bags that you have on hand.

CHOCOLATE ÉCLAIRS

These éclairs are light as air and are really quite easy to master and whip up in no time. A piping bag is essential to getting the recognisable éclair shape but you could also use a ziplock bag with the end cut off. Fill the éclairs with fresh fruit, or turn the coconut cream into chocolate coconut cream by adding 1 tbsp of raw cacao powder, get creative!

MAKES 6

1 cup (250ml) water
80g/3 oz butter, cubed
1 cup (130g) brown rice flour
3 free range eggs, whisked
1 serve of whisked coconut cream (page 65)
Fresh strawberries to serve
1 serve chocolate ganache (page 133)

Pre-heat the oven to 200°C/400°F. In a small saucepan melt the butter with the water and bring to the boil over a medium heat. Reduce the heat to low and add the flour, using a spoon to stir until the mixture forms a ball and comes away from the side of the pan. Remove from the heat and leave to cool for 2-3 minutes.

Add one egg at a time to the roux, mixing between additions until the mixture is glossy. Using a piping bag fitted with a round tip, pipe the mixture into long lines on an oven tray lined with baking paper. Space the lines at least 2 inches apart, as they will expand when cooking. As an optional extra, brush the top of each profiterole with a dab of milk or whisked egg. Bake in the oven for 25-30 minutes until puffed. Turn the oven off; remove the tray and using a skewer poke a small hole in each éclair to release steam. Return the tray to the oven while the oven is cooling down, leaving the oven door ajar.

While the profiteroles are cooling make the whipped coconut cream following the recipe on page 65.

Once the éclairs are at room temperature, slice each in half and fill with the whipped coconut cream and sliced fresh strawberries. Prepare the chocolate ganache following the instructions on page 133. Top each éclair with a spoonful of ganache and enjoy!

CHICKPEA CHOCOLATE CHIP COOKIES

The sweetness in this recipe comes from the dark chocolate, use only the best quality and the darker the better. If you'd rather omit the chocolate, you can add chopped walnuts or cacao nibs for something different. If using either of these you may want to add a small amount of sweetener to the dough such as rice malt syrup, maple syrup or raw honey. As these cookies don't have the amount of sugars, stabilisers or artificial ingredients as store-bought cookies their shelf life is considerably less. Bake cookies as needed and freeze the rest of the dough.

MAKES 12

400g/14 oz cooked chickpeas
⅔ cup (90g) brown rice flour
1 tsp baking powder
⅓ cup (80ml) coconut oil, melted
2 tbsp milk (nut milk can be substituted)
1 tsp vanilla powder
1 tsp cinnamon
1 tsp nutmeg
2 tsp sea salt
⅔ cup (170g) dark chocolate chips

Preheat the oven to 180°C/350°F.

Rinse and drain the chickpeas from the can then add to the bowl of a food processor fitted with the S blade attachment. Puree until smooth then add the flour and baking powder and pulse.

Scrape down the sides of the bowl then add the coconut oil, milk, vanilla powder, cinnamon, nutmeg and sea salt. Pulse until combined. Stir through the chocolate chips.

Roll the dough into small balls or use an ice cream scoop to create even-sized cookies and then place on an oven tray lined with baking paper. Use the back of a fork to press each ball down slightly. Bake for 20 minutes and store in an airtight container.

LET'S DATE CAKE

This moist date and coconut cake can be made in a small tin and sandwiched together with the whipped coconut milk to create a cute mini cake or can be baked in a larger tin to create one large cake and topped with the cream, both are perfect to share.

SERVES 4

250g/9 oz fresh Medjool dates, pitted
1 cup (80g) shredded coconut
½ cup (125ml) melted butter
½ cup (125ml) coconut milk
5 free range eggs, separated
¾ cup (75g) almond meal
1 tsp ground cinnamon
1 tsp ground ginger
1 tsp vanilla powder

COCONUT FROSTING
1 cup (250ml) coconut milk, refrigerated overnight
Pinch of vanilla powder

Preheat the oven to 170°C/320°F. Grease one large spring form tin or four smaller tins. If you only have one small tin, you can make the cake layers in batches. Place a circle of greaseproof paper on the bottom of the tin to remove the cake easier when cooked.

Blitz the dates and shredded coconut in a food processor before adding the melted butter and coconut milk.

Using a stand mixer or a hand-held mixer beat the egg yolks with the cinnamon, ginger and vanilla until just thicker in consistency, approximately 2-4 minutes.

In a large mixing bowl combine the egg yolk mixture with the date mixture then stir the almond meal through gently.

Beat the egg whites in a clean bowl until stiff peaks form. Fold the beaten egg whites gently through the rest of the mixture.

Pour batter into the prepared tin and bake in the oven for 35-45 minutes or until an inserted skewer comes out clean. Once cooked, let cool for 10 minutes in the tin before turning out onto a wire rack and leaving to cool completely.

Prepare the whipped coconut frosting by whisking (either by hand or using a stand mixer) the coconut milk with a pinch of vanilla powder until thickened. It's best to refrigerate the coconut milk overnight to help it thicken when whisking, however refrigerating for a period of four hours or more will also help. You can replace the coconut milk with unsweetened whipped cream if desired.

Sandwich layers of the cake together with the frosting or pile it atop the cake and garnish with fresh strawberries.

CHOCOLATE DIPPED MERINGUE KISSES

These bite-size treats are easy to make and customise to your tastes or what you have on hand. You can stir hazelnut meal through the meringue prior to baking, or you can flavour them with raw cacao, crushed freeze-dried berries or vanilla powder. Without the white sugar I find these meringues don't last as long so are best enjoyed on the day and shared around.

MAKES 12

2 free range egg whites, at room temperature
½ cup (125ml) maple or rice malt syrup
¼ tsp ground cinnamon
Pinch of sea salt

100g/3.5 oz dark chocolate, 70% cacao+
½ tsp vanilla powder

Preheat the oven to 100°C/200°F.
    Prepare a double boiler on the stovetop by bringing 1 cup (250ml) of water to the boil in a saucepan then reducing the heat to low and placing a small bowl over the top of the simmering water.
    In the small bowl add the egg whites, sweetener and salt and whisk for 5 minutes until the egg whites begin to thicken. Transfer the mixture to the bowl of a stand mixer or use hand beaters to whisk the egg whites to stiff peaks, a further 5 minutes.
    Place the meringue mixture into a piping bag and pipe medium-sized rounds onto an oven tray lined with baking paper. Bake in the oven for 1½ hours or until crispy throughout – you can test this by inserting a skewer into the base of a meringue. Remove from the oven and cool on a wire rack.
    Melt the chocolate with the vanilla powder until smooth and glossy. Dip the base of each meringue into the melted chocolate and turn to allow the excess to drip off.
    Optional extras include dipping the meringue in crushed nuts or shredded coconut, or sandwich two meringues together with the melted chocolate. Store in an airtight container, the meringues lose their crunch quickly so are best enjoyed within 2 days of baking.

NUTTY FUDGE

Oh fudge, how do I love thee? Let me count the ways. I love that you're incredibly easy to make, that you only require one bowl and minimal clean up afterwards, and that you set in the fridge in half an hour, allowing me enough time to choose a movie, make a cup of tea and hop into my pyjamas before slicing you into squares and devouring you without any remorse.

MAKES 12

1 cup (270g) smooth nut butter of choice
½ cup (125ml) coconut oil, melted
1 tbsp rice malt syrup
½ cup (60g) raw cacao powder
½ cup (85g) macadamia nuts

Combine the nut butter, coconut oil, rice malt syrup and raw cacao powder in a bowl, whisk until smooth.
    Roughly chop the macadamia nuts and stir through the fudge batter.
    Line a shallow brownie tin with baking paper and pour the batter in, smoothing into the corners with a knife. Place in the fridge to set for about 30 minutes before slicing into squares. You can wrap the fudge in squares of greaseproof paper or keep in the tin, store in the fridge until ready to eat.

BOUNTY PATTIES

Coconut is one of my favourite ingredients to work with; it adds a natural sweetness to food and is so easy to work with. It's a given then that a spin on the classic Bounty (Mounds) bar appears in this section. I like to make these as small patties or rounds, kind of like the after dinner mint that was all the rage in 80s and 90s entertaining. You could also make these as bars by pushing the mixture into a shallow brownie tin then cutting into strips when set and coating in the chocolate.

MAKES 10

PATTIES
2 cups (160g) unsweetened shredded coconut
Pinch of sea salt
½ tsp vanilla powder
¼ cup (60ml) coconut oil, melted
¼ cup (60ml) cacao butter, melted
2 tbsp raw honey (or maple syrup for a milder flavour)

RAW CHOCOLATE
¼ cup (60ml) coconut oil, melted
¼ cup (60ml) cacao butter, melted
¼ cup (30g) raw cacao powder
Pinch of sea salt
1 tbsp sweetener of choice

*Alternatively use melted good quality, 70%+ dark chocolate to coat the patties

In the bowl of a food processor add the shredded coconut, salt and vanilla powder. Blend on high until the coconut breaks down into a texture you're happy with. You can have the patty filling chunky or blend it down to a smoother paste. Stir though the melted coconut oil and cacao butter as well as your sweetener of choice through the coconut.

Line a tray with baking paper. Take spoonfuls of the mixture and roll into balls in your hands. Place the balls on the tray and push down gently to flatten into a patty shape. Continue until all of the mixture has been used. Place the tray in the fridge for 1 hour or until firm.

Prepare the chocolate coating by combining the melted coconut oil, cacao butter and raw cacao in a bowl. Whisk until there are no lumps then stir through the sea salt and sweetener of choice. If using dark chocolate, melt the chocolate in a bowl over a saucepan of simmering water, add a pinch of sea salt if you'd like.

Remove the patties from the fridge and coat in the chocolate. Place a tray under a wire rack and set the patties on it after dipping. You can sit the patties on a fork to lower into the chocolate or dip them in using your fingers. Alternatively, to just cover the top of the patties, pour the chocolate over the top of them. When you have dipped all of the patties, place the tray in the fridge to set. Store the patties in the fridge in an airtight container.

Mix up the basic recipe by adding a dried fruit of choice to the coconut mixture. Try cherries, goji berries or blueberries to add sweetness and a chewy texture. Flavour the raw chocolate with different spices to alter the overall flavour of the patties – try cinnamon or ginger.

ROSE + COCONUT MOUSSE

This simple mousse is light as air and not overly sweet, a perfect dessert to end a meal without weighing you down further. You can layer the mousse in cups with the chopped pistachios and raspberries or customise it to your tastes by adding nuts, other fruit or dark chocolate shavings over the top.

SERVES 2

1 cup (250ml) coconut milk
2 free range egg whites
1-2 tsp rose water
½ tsp vanilla powder
25g/1 oz shelled pistachios, finely chopped
Fresh raspberries, to serve

Chill the coconut milk overnight in the fridge.

When ready to prepare the mousse, whisk the egg whites until stiff peaks form.

In a separate bowl, whisk the coconut milk until thickened. Fold the egg whites through the coconut milk with the rose water and vanilla powder. Add more rose water as needed to suit your taste.

Divide the mixture evenly between glasses or bowls and place in the fridge for 1-2 hours to set. Serve each mousse with a sprinkling of finely chopped pistachios and fresh raspberries.

PISTACHIO, ROSE + TAHINI CRISPIES

This spin on the childhood favourite, rice crispy squares, replaces sugary marshmallow with tahini and creamy coconut butter. It takes its flavour inspiration from the often-overlooked Turkish delight, blending rose water and pistachios with chewy goji berries to create a sweet and perfumed treat. If rose water and Turkish delight aren't your jam, the recipe works perfectly well without it.

SERVES 10

1½ cups (60g) puffed brown rice
1 cup (40g) puffed quinoa
⅓ cup (40g) shelled pistachios
½ cup (55g) goji berries
½ cup (125g) hulled tahini
½ cup (125ml) coconut butter, melted
2 tbsp coconut oil
1-2 tbsp rose water
½ cup (125ml) rice malt syrup
Pinch of sea salt

In a bowl combine the puffed brown rice and puffed quinoa. Roughly chop the pistachios and add to the bowl.

In a small saucepan add the tahini, coconut butter and coconut oil, heat until melted and combined. Take off the heat and stir through the rose water, rice malt syrup and sea salt.

Pour the mixture into a tin lined with baking paper and smooth out the top as much as possible. Chill in the refrigerator to set then remove from the tin and slice into squares. Store in the fridge.

CRISPY CARAMEL CUPS

The peanut butter cup has had its day, it's time for that treat to move over and make way for gooey caramel, crispy quinoa and silky raw chocolate. These addictive morsels are Real Food certified, not a skerrick of fake ingredients in sight. Date caramel, wholesome quinoa and cacao-rich homemade chocolate are the perfect blend of flavours and textures; you'll be wondering why you didn't combine them before now.

MAKES 12 SMALL CUPS

CRISPY QUINOA
1½ tsp extra virgin coconut oil, melted
½ cup (90g) cooked quinoa

DATE CARAMEL
6 Medjool dates, pitted
1 tsp vanilla powder
1 tbsp coconut oil
Pinch of sea salt

RAW CHOCOLATE
½ cup (125ml) extra virgin coconut oil, melted
½ cup (60g) raw cacao powder
1 tbsp maple or rice malt syrup
Pinch of sea salt

Preheat the oven to 180°C/350°F and line an oven tray with baking paper. Mix the melted coconut oil through the cooked quinoa then spread the quinoa out into an even layer on the tray. Bake for 20 minutes, keeping an eye on it and stirring if needed. Once the quinoa is crispy, remove the tray from the oven and set aside to cool.

Prepare the caramel by soaking the dates in boiling water for 10 minutes. Drain then add the pitted dates to the bowl of a food processor with the vanilla powder, coconut oil and sea salt. Blitz until a smooth caramel-coloured mixture comes together.

Prepare the raw chocolate by whisking the coconut oil, cacao powder, rice malt syrup and sea salt together in a bowl until combined.

To make the cups, lay out mini patty pans on a tray or plate. Use a tablespoon or small scoop to pour the base layer of chocolate into each patty pan. Place the tray in the fridge for 5-10 minutes to harden. Remove the tray from the refrigerator and add 1 tsp of the crispy quinoa and 1 tsp of the date caramel to each patty pan. Use the back of the teaspoon to push down on the caramel and create an even layer. Use the remaining chocolate mixture to pour over the top of the caramel. Return the tray to the fridge for 5-10 minutes to set the top layer of chocolate and store in the fridge until ready to eat. You can store any leftover crispy quinoa in a ziplock bag or airtight container for up to a week or freeze.

Turn the crispy caramel cups into tasty nut butter cups by using your favourite nut butter in place of the date caramel. For another variation, try substituting tahini for the caramel, and add a sprinkling of crushed sunflower seeds to each cup for a nut-free alternative.

TOP DECK
PANNA COTTA

Panna cotta is a great dessert because you can make it as sweet or tart as you like. You can use coconut milk, almond or dairy milk to customise for dietary needs and flavour. You can sweeten with rice malt syrup, maple syrup or raw honey.

SERVES 6

1½ cups (375ml) coconut milk
⅓ cup (80ml) rice malt syrup
Pinch of vanilla powder
1½ tbsp raw cacao powder
¼ cup (60ml) water
1 tbsp gelatine
Dark chocolate (70%+ cocoa)
  shavings for serving (optional)

In a small saucepan heat half the coconut milk with the rice malt syrup, vanilla powder and water over a low heat until combined. Whisk if needed to remove lumps. Remove the pan from the heat and divide the mixture into two bowls. In one bowl add the raw cacao, whisk until smooth.

Sprinkle half the gelatine over the top of the chocolate mixture and stir or whisk until dissolved. Fill the bottom of 6 ramekins, jars or moulds with the chocolate mixture and place in the refrigerator to set for 2 hours.

Once the bottom layer of panna cotta has set, gently heat the vanilla mixture in a small pan, stir through the gelatine until dissolved and set aside to cool for 5 minutes. Pour the cooled vanilla mixture over the top of the chocolate in each vessel. Place in the refrigerator to set for 2 hours.

Serve the panna cottas with shavings of dark chocolate on top if desired.

VANILLA CUPCAKES WITH CHOCOLATE FROSTING

A cover model needs to be tempting to a prospective audience, she must make the book or magazine inviting and alluring, perhaps she also makes them slightly envious of her curves or flawless frosting, of the glossy ganache, the light-as-air sponge, and the juicy fruit sitting atop her head. Looks are one thing but it's what's inside that counts, and this vanilla cupcake with chocolate frosting delivers on taste as well.

MAKES 12

½ cup (125ml) coconut butter, melted
1½ cups (375ml) coconut milk
½ cup (125ml) rice malt syrup
1 vanilla bean pod
6 free range eggs
¾ cup (100g) coconut flour

CHOCOLATE FROSTING
3 tbsp coconut oil, melted
3 tbsp coconut milk
3 tbsp maple syrup or sweetener of choice
3 tbsp raw cacao powder
1 tbsp Dutch press cocoa
¼ tsp vanilla powder

Fresh fruit, nuts, seeds or coconut to decorate

Preheat the oven to 160°C/320°F.

In a saucepan combine the coconut butter, coconut milk and rice malt syrup together with the seeds from the vanilla bean pod. Take off the heat and set aside.

Separate the egg yolks and whites. Whisk the whites to stiff peaks and set aside. Stir the egg yolks through the cooled coconut mixture followed by the coconut flour.

Lastly, fold the whipped egg whites through the mixture until just combined, taking care not to lose too much air from the mixture.

Use an ice cream scoop to evenly distribute the batter between 12 cupcake liners and bake in the oven for 30 minutes or until an inserted skewer comes out clean. Remove from the oven and cool on a wire rack.

Prepare the frosting by whisking together the coconut oil, coconut milk, rice malt syrup, raw cacao powder, Dutch press cocoa and vanilla powder until smooth and glossy. Dip each cupcake into the frosting and turn to allow the excess to drip off. Alternatively, place the frosting in the fridge for 5 minutes to firm up then spread over the top of the cupcakes. Top each cupcake with your fruit of choice, such as pomegranate seeds or orange segments, shredded coconut or chopped nuts.

Using Dutch press cocoa in addition to the raw cacao will give the chocolate ganache a greater depth of flavour but you can just use raw cacao for similar results or use melted good quality dark chocolate (minimum 70% cocoa) mixed with cream for a traditional ganache or coconut milk for a dairy-free option.

Once you switch to a Real Food life you will find treats you once enjoyed aren't the best choices anymore. Store-bought chocolate bars are often filled with excess sugar and when you do find a brand that ticks the boxes you're forced to settle with the limited selection of flavours they produce. Invest in a cheap chocolate mould and go to town making your own delectable dark chocolate treats.

TOASTED COCONUT + PUFFED QUINOA WHITE CHOCOLATE BLOCK

MAKES 1 LARGE BLOCK

4 tbsp cacao butter
3 tbsp coconut oil
3 tbsp rice malt syrup, honey
 or maple syrup
2 tbsp unhulled tahini
1 tsp vanilla powder
½ cup (40g) unsweetened shredded
 coconut
⅓ cup (10g) puffed quinoa

In a small saucepan melt the cacao butter and coconut oil over a low heat. As soon as the mixture turns liquid remove it from the heat and whisk in your sweetener of choice, the tahini and vanilla powder.

In a small pan, dry toast the shredded coconut until golden in colour.

Sprinkle the toasted coconut and the puffed quinoa over the bottom of the chocolate mould, or use cupcake liners to make small treats. Pour the chocolate mix over the top and place in the freezer to set for at least one hour. Store in the fridge.

ACAI BERRY + POMEGRANATE DARK CHOCOLATE BLOCK

MAKES 1 LARGE BLOCK

4 tbsp cacao butter
3 tbsp coconut oil
3 tbsp rice malt syrup, honey
 or maple syrup
¾ cup (90g) raw cacao powder
2 tbsp acai berry powder
1 tsp vanilla powder
Seeds from ½ a pomegranate
2 tbsp freeze dried raspberries,
 crushed (optional)

In a small saucepan melt the cacao butter and coconut oil over a low heat. As soon as the mixture turns liquid remove it from the heat and whisk in your sweetener of choice.

Sift in the raw cacao powder and whisk until the mixture is smooth and glossy. Stir through the acai berry powder, vanilla powder and pomegranate seeds.

Pour the mixture into a chocolate block mould or mould of choice, fill right to the top and place in the fridge to set for at least 1 hour.

When ready, pop the chocolate out of the mould and scatter crushed freeze dried raspberries over the top of the block. Tear off a large piece of aluminium foil and wrap the chocolate in it, as you would see a store bought block. Store in the fridge and snap off a square whenever the mood strikes you.

CHOCOLATE MARSHMALLOW WHEELS

This recipe has quite a few steps but the end product is well worth the time investment in the kitchen. The Wagon Wheel biscuit is a favourite of mine from childhood and when you break down the components it's quite easy to make a Real Food version at home.

SERVES 6

ALMOND SHORTBREAD BASE
1½ cups (195g) brown rice flour
1 cup (100g) almond meal
Pinch of sea salt
1 tsp vanilla powder
2 tbsp rice malt syrup
150g/5 oz grass fed butter, melted
¼ cup (60ml) cold water

STRAWBERRY-RASPBERRY JAM
1 cup (150g) strawberries, fresh
  or frozen
1 cup (150g) raspberries, fresh
  or frozen
1 tbsp water
½ tbsp grass fed gelatine
*Or use the strawberry cinnamon
  chia jam on page 60

MARSHMALLOW
½ (125ml) cup water
1 tbsp grass fed gelatine
½ cup (125ml) rice malt syrup
½ tsp vanilla powder
½ tsp sea salt

250g/7 oz dark chocolate for coating

Preheat the oven to 160°C/320°F. Sift the rice flour, almond meal, salt and vanilla powder into a large bowl and add the butter and rice malt syrup. Stir through the water and mix until a dough forms. Add more almond meal if the dough is too wet and press into a baking paper lined tin (to make a slice) or roll out and use a round cookie cutter to make the biscuits. You can also roll portions of the dough into rounds and gently press down to create the biscuit shape. As the dough is delicate you may find it easier to press it into a shallow tin,

refrigerate it for 10 minutes then cut the rounds out of that. Carefully place the biscuits on an oven tray lined with baking paper and bake for 15 minutes or until golden brown.

To make the jam, add the strawberries, raspberries and water to a small pan, heat over medium until the berries begin releasing juice. Remove the pan from the heat and whisk through the gelatine and vanilla powder. You can keep the jam chunky or puree it a little for a smoother texture. Set the mixture aside to cool while you make the marshmallow.

In a small bowl or the bowl of a stand mixer, combine ¼ cup (60ml) of water with the gelatine. In a small saucepan combine ¼ cup (60ml) of water with the rice malt syrup and salt and bring to the boil over medium heat. Using a candy thermometer, bring the mixture to soft ball point or 118°C/244°F. Remove from the heat and slowly pour the rice malt syrup mixture into the gelatine and water mixture in the bowl. Whisk for approximately 10 minutes with the mixer on slow until fluffy and sticky.

While the marshmallow is whisking, lay half the shortbread cookies out. When the marshmallow is done, quickly spoon a small amount on top of each cookie, add 2 tsp of jam then place the remaining cookies on top and press gently together to seal.

Melt the dark chocolate in a bowl over a saucepan of simmering water until smooth and glossy, set aside to cool slightly. Dip the cookies into the melted chocolate, turning to allow any excess to run off. Place a wire rack over a tray or piece of baking paper and lay the coated cookies on the tray for the chocolate to harden. Store in the fridge or cupboard in an airtight container.

PEACHES WITH GOAT CHEESE + CRISPY PROSCUITTO

This recipe perfectly balances the savoury and sweet, pairing juicy in-season peaches with creamy goat cheese and salty prosciutto. Recipes such as this remind us that desserts don't need to be overly sweet or complicated. You can substitute other fruits for the peaches such as plums, apricots or even watermelon.

SERVES 2

25/1 oz butter, cubed
2 peaches, any variety
½ tsp ground cinnamon
½ tsp nutmeg
½ tsp ground cardamom
½ tsp ground ginger
50g/2 oz goat cheese
2-4 thin slices of proscuitto

Preheat the oven to 180°C/350°F.

Slice the peaches in half and remove the pits. In a pan over medium heat add the butter followed by the peaches, skin side down.

Mix the spices together in a small bowl then sprinkle over the peaches while they're cooking. Cook for 5 minutes each side until the flesh begins to soften. Meanwhile, heat a small pan and cook the proscuitto until crisp. Drain on paper towel then roughly chop or add to the bowl of a food processor and blitz.

Remove the peaches from the pan, spoon the goat cheese into each peach (where the pit was removed) and top with proscuitto.

COFFEE PUDDING WITH SALTED CARAMEL CHIA CRUNCH

Combine coffee and dessert and you probably think of tiramisu, this coffee treat comes together in a flash and is a great way to use up that leftover coffee from the morning. The salted caramel chia crunch can be omitted but adds a nice variation of texture.

MAKES 4

PUDDING
½ cup (125ml) strong brewed coffee, chilled
2 tbsp hulled tahini
1 tsp vanilla powder
1 cup (250ml) almond milk
1 tbsp coconut oil
1 cup (125g) cashews, soaked overnight

SALTED CARAMEL CHIA CRUNCH
¼ cup (40g) chia seeds
1 cup (250ml) maple syrup
1 tsp sea salt

Make the pudding by whisking the coffee, tahini, vanilla powder, almond milk and coconut oil in a bowl until combined.

Rinse the soaked cashews in fresh water, drain then add to the bowl of a food processor fitted with an S blade and blitz on high until the cashews form a paste/butter. Add the coffee mixture and blitz until all combined. Distribute the pudding mixture between ramekins or glasses and place in the fridge for 1 hour.

Make the salted caramel chia crunch by spreading the chia seeds evenly over an oven tray lined with baking paper.

In a saucepan heat the maple syrup to soft crack stage (143°C/290°F). Prop a candy thermometer against the internal side of the pan to keep an eye on the temperature. Once it has reached this, stir through the sea salt then pour over the chia seeds on the oven tray, using a spatula to scrape it all out of the pan. Set the tray aside to cool and harden then break into shards and serve on top of the puddings.

ALMOND + MACADAMIA CARAMEL SLICE

Gooey caramel is hard to pass up, especially when paired with a macadamia crust and a dark chocolate topping. This slice is perfect to make for afternoon tea or a casual dessert and while it uses dates instead of white sugar, it is still a sweet treat to be enjoyed occasionally and shared around.

SERVES 6-8

BASE
1 cup (100g) almond meal
1 cup (150g) macadamia nuts
⅓ cup (80ml) melted butter
   or coconut oil

FILLING
2 cups (340g) fresh Medjool dates
½ cup (125ml) coconut oil, melted
2 tbsp hulled tahini
¼ cup (60ml) coconut milk
2 tbsp coconut butter

TOPPING
200g/7 oz dark chocolate (minimum
   70% cocoa) or raw chocolate
   (page 149)

Process the almond meal and macadamia nuts in the bowl of a food processor until a fine crumb forms. Add the butter and pulse until combined. Line a shallow brownie tin with baking paper and press the base mixture into the tin, pushing down until level and compact. Place the tin in the fridge while you prepare the filling.

For the caramel filling, soak the dates in boiling water for 10 minutes then remove the pits and add the dates to the bowl of a food processor along with the coconut oil, tahini, coconut milk and coconut butter. Blitz until combined and creamy. Pour the caramel topping over the base and use a spatula to even the surface. Return the tin to the fridge for at least 1 hour to set.

Melt the dark chocolate or pre-pare the raw chocolate following the instructions on page 149. Let the mixture cool slightly then pour over the caramel slice and spread evenly. Return the tin to the fridge to set then cut the slice into squares. Store in the fridge.

CHERRY BLACK BEAN BROWNIES

Using black beans is the secret weapon of this recipe to keep the brownies soft, fudgy and delicious while the cherries add a tartness that compliments the chocolate perfectly. Brownies are the perfect treat to enjoy in bite-size squares, and you can easily change the flavour profile of the recipe by substituting the cherries for nuts or another fruit.

MAKES 12

150g/5 oz butter, melted
½ cup (60g) raw cacao powder
Pinch of vanilla powder
1 cup (170g) cooked black beans
3 free range eggs
½ cup (50g) almond meal/flour
1 cup (110g) fresh or frozen cherries,
   pitted
50-75g/2-3 oz dark chocolate
   (70+ cocoa)
1 tsp sea salt

Preheat the oven to 160°C/320°F.

In a food processor add the melted butter, raw cacao and vanilla powders, black beans, eggs and almond flour, blitz until combined. Fold through half the cherries, reserving the remaining half for the top of the brownies.

Roughly chop the dark chocolate, add half to the brownie batter and reserve half to top the brownies with. Sprinkle ½ teaspoon of the sea salt into the batter and stir to combine.

Pour the batter into a brownie or baking tin lined with greaseproof paper. If you want tall brownies, opt for a smaller tin with higher walls, or use a flatter, longer tin for thinner treats. Smooth the top of the mixture in the tin and dot the surface with the remaining cherries and dark chocolate. Sprinkle the remaining ½ teaspoon of sea salt evenly over the top of the brownie. Bake in the oven for 25-30 minutes or until an inserted skewer comes out clean.

Index

SOMETHING SWEET

Happy cooking!

CONVERSION TABLES

Converting Ounces to Grams	
OUNCES	**GRAMS**
1 ounce	30 grams
2 ounces	60 grams
3 ounces	85 grams
4 ounces	115 grams
5 ounces	140 grams
6 ounces	180 grams
7 ounces	200 grams
8 ounces	225 grams
9 ounces	250 grams
10 ounces	285 grams
11 ounces	300 grams
12 ounces	340 grams
13 ounces	370 grams
14 ounces	400 grams
15 ounces	425 grams
16 ounces	450 grams

Converting Quarts to Litres	
QUARTS	**LITRES**
1 cup (¼ quart)	¼ litre
1 pint (½ quart)	½ litre
1 quart	1 litre
2 quarts	2 litres
2½ quarts	2½ litres
3 quarts	2¾ litres
4 quarts	3¾ litres
5 quarts	4¾ litres
6 quarts	5½ litres
7 quarts	6½ litres
8 quarts	7½ litres

Converting Pounds to Grams and Kilograms	
POUNDS	**GRAMS; KILOGRAMS**
1 pound	450 grams
1½ pounds	675 grams
2 pounds	900 grams
2½ pounds	1,125 grams; 1¼ kilograms
3 pounds	1,350 grams
3½ pounds	1,500 grams; 1½ kilograms
4 pounds	1,800 grams
4½ pounds	2 kilograms
5 pounds	2¼ kilograms
5½ pounds	2½ kilograms
6 pounds	2¾ kilograms
6½ pounds	3 kilograms
7 pounds	3¼ kilograms
7½ pounds	3½ kilograms
8 pounds	3¾ kilograms

Converting Fahrenheit to Celsius	
FAHRENHEIT	**CELSIUS**
170	77
180	82
190	88
200	95
225	110
250	120
300	150
325	165
350	180
375	190
400	205
425	220
450	230
475	245
500	260